Minutes a Day-Mastery for a Lifetime!

Common Core Mathematics 2

2nd Semester

Nancy L. McGraw
Donna M. Mazzola
Nancy Tondy
Christopher Backs
Diane Dillon
Lori Lender

Bright Ideas Press, LLC
Cleveland, OH

Simple Solutions

Common Core Mathematics 2

2nd Semester

Printed in the United States of America

ISBN: 978-1-60873-155-8

The writers of *Simple Solutions* Common Core Mathematics aligned the series in accordance with information from the following:

National Governors Association Center for Best Practices, Council of Chief State School Officers. *Common Core State Standards, Mathematics*. National Governors Association Center for Best Practices, Council of Chief State School Officers, Washington, D.C.: 2010.

United States coin images from the United States Mint.

Cover Design: Dan Mazzola
Editor: Rebecca Toukonen

Dear Student:

This workbook will give you the opportunity to practice skills you have learned in previous grades. By practicing these skills each day, you will gain confidence in your math ability.

Using this workbook will help you understand math concepts more easily. For many of you, using *Simple Solutions* will give you a more positive attitude towards math in general.

In order for this program to help you be successful, it is extremely important that you do a lesson every day. It is also important that you check your answers and ask your teacher for help with the problems you didn't understand or that you did incorrectly.

Simple Solutions: Minutes a day—Mastery for a Lifetime!

When you are finished with this book, please recycle it if you can.

Lesson #73

1. 856 – 234 = ?

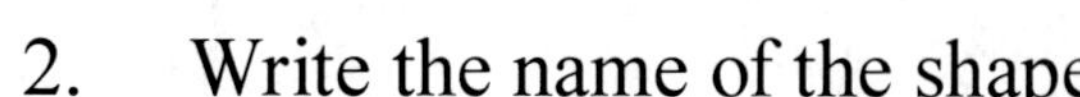

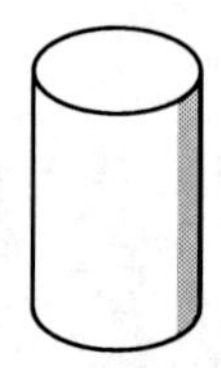

2. Write the name of the shape.

   cone sphere cylinder

3. What number does the symbol stand for? 55 – ♥ = 50

4. Write the base-ten number for five hundred seventy-two.

5. Fill in the sign to make this sentence true. 964 ◯ 694

6. Which is longer, five inches or five feet?

7. 538 + 361 = ?

8. Which circle is <u>not</u> divided into two equal halves? Draw it.

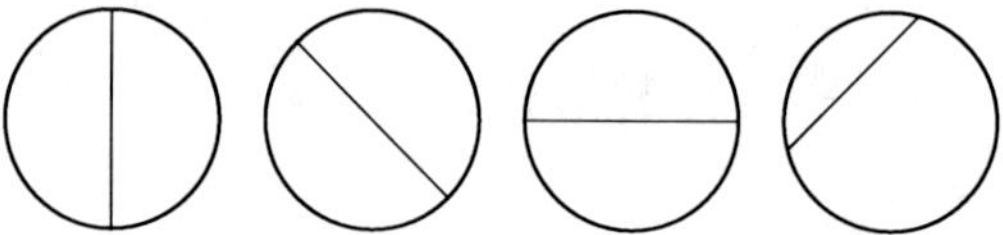

9. \$16.45 + \$22.52 = ?

10. Which of the shapes are quadrilaterals? Draw them in the box.

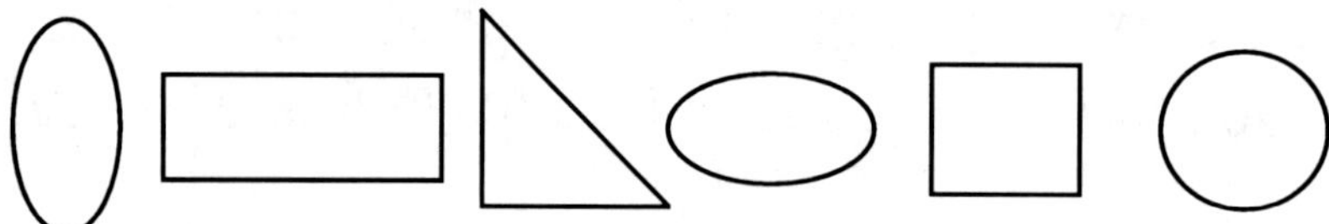

11. Write the number as a base-ten numeral. 60 + 6 + 100.

12. What number is 100 less than 550?

13. 4 + 7 = ?

14. Write your answers in inches.

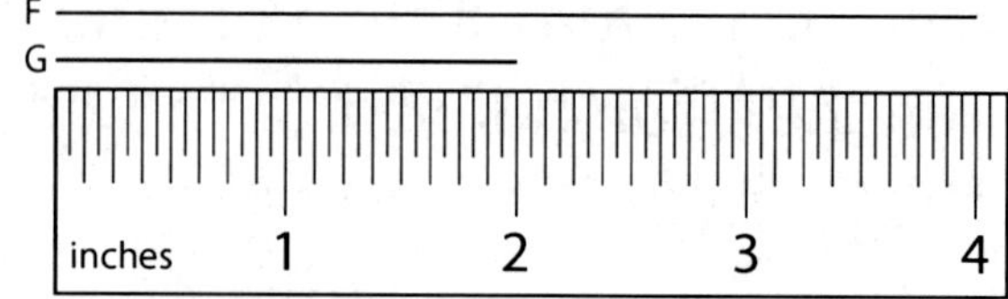

- How long is line F?
- How long is line G?
- How much shorter is line G than line F?
- What is the sum of the two lengths?

15. If Ellen buys a bag of chips for 35¢, and a bottle of soda pop for 85¢, and a pack of gum for 30¢, how much money did she spend?

1. 2.NBT.7	2. 1.G.2	3. 2.OA.1
4. 2.NBT.3	5. 2.NBT.4	6. 2.MD.3
7. 2.NBT.7	8. 2.G.3	9. 2.MD.8
10. 2.G.1	11. 2.NBT.3	12. 2.NBT.8
13. 2.OA.2	14. 2.MD.4	15. 2.MD.8

Lesson #74

1. Which rectangle is not divided into two equal halves? Draw it.

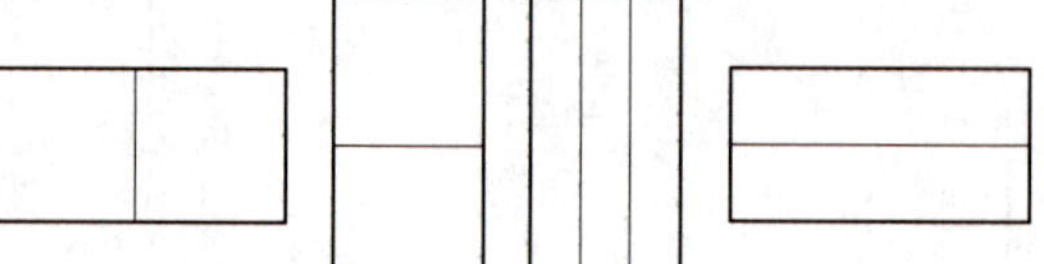

2. 23 + 44 + 31 = ?

3. Find Pencil A on page 153 of your Hands-On pages. Measure its length to the nearest centimeter.

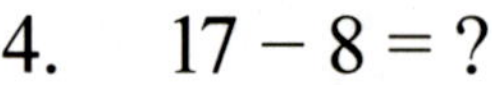

4. 17 − 8 = ?

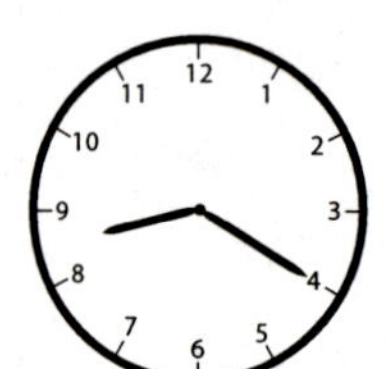

5. What time is it?

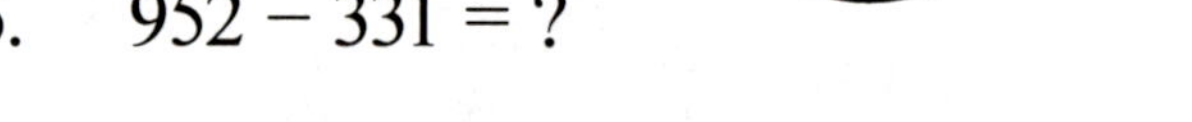

6. 952 − 331 = ?

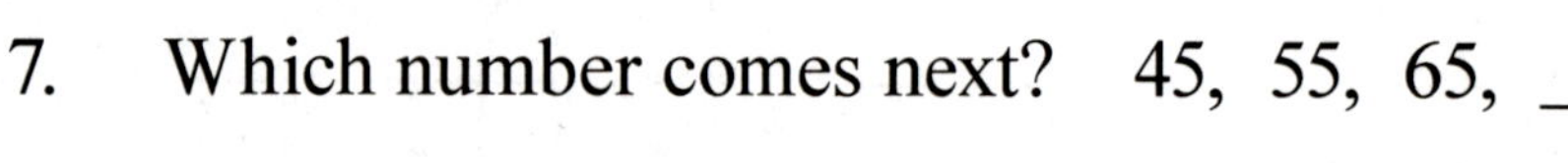

7. Which number comes next? 45, 55, 65, ______

8. Is 46 closer to 40 or 50?

9. What number does the symbol stand for? 32 – 30 = ♠

10. Order these numbers from greatest to least. 832, 245, 916, 740

11. How many cents do you have if you have four nickels, four pennies, and one quarter?

12. Fill in the sign to make this sentence true. 318 ○ 183

13. There were 37 boats in the dock and another 15 out on the lake. How many boats were there in all?

14. Would the Statue of Liberty be closer to 300 feet or 300 inches tall?

15. How many cans were collected in all?

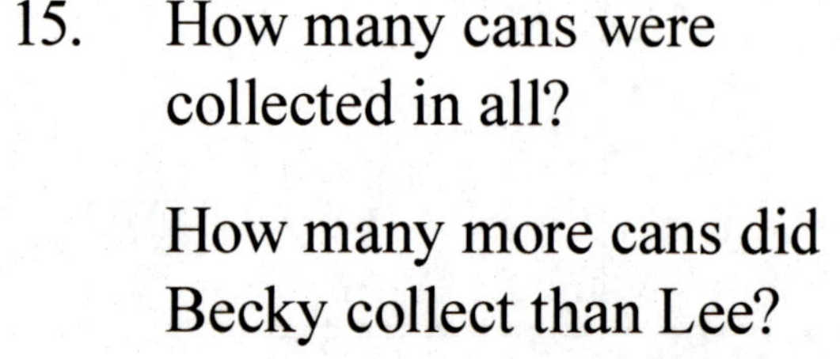

How many more cans did Becky collect than Lee?

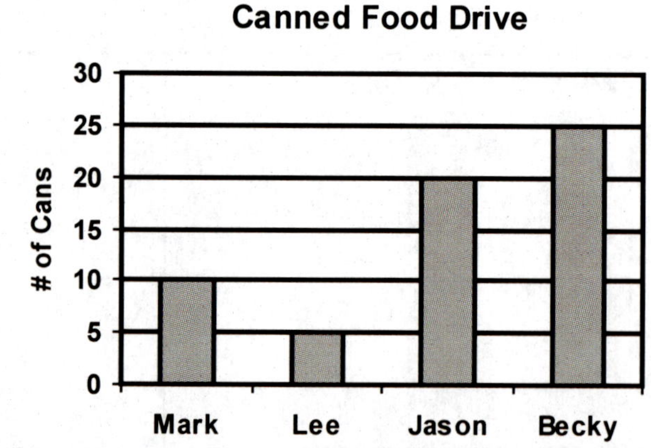

1. 2.G.3	2. 2.NBT.6	3. 2.MD.3
4. 2.OA.2	5. 2.MD.7	6. 2.NBT.7
7. 2.NBT.2	8. 3.NBT.1 (Prep)	9. 2.OA.1
10. 2.NBT.4	11. 2.MD.8	12. 2.NBT.4
13. 2.OA.1	14. 2.MD.10	15. 2.MD.10

Lesson #75

1. If you have five quarters, do you have more or less than a dollar?

2. Find the worm on page 152 of your Hands-On pages. Measure its length to the nearest inch.

3. Fill in the missing numbers. 80, 90, ____, 110, ____

4. Which is the best tool for measuring the length of your desk?

A) 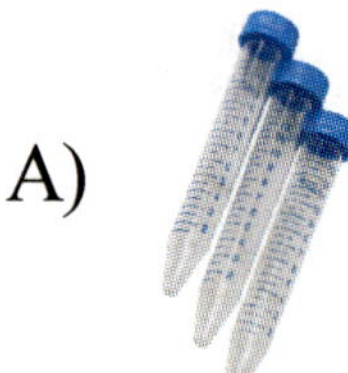　B) 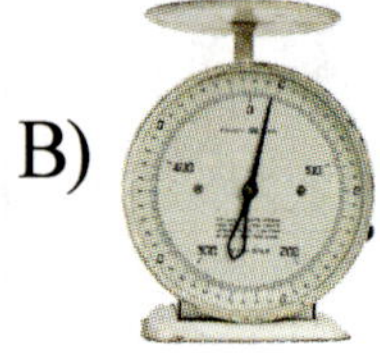　C) 

5. Mentally add 100. 425, 525, _____, _____, _____

6. 56 + 44 = ?

7. Write the time. 

8. 957 − 425 = ?

9. Would Reba choose a walking stick 1 centimeter or 1 meter long?

10. $33.25 + $14.32 = ?

11. Is the number of ants even or odd? Count by 2s.

12. 8 + 7 + 5 = ?

13. What base-ten number is this? 600 + 30 + 3

14. Would Jeff need tennis shoes that were 8 inches or 8 feet long?

15. Trina brought 36 cupcakes to the bake sale. She sold 11 cupcakes before lunch and she sold 13 cupcakes after lunch. How many of Trina's cupcakes were left over?

1. 2.MD.8	2. 2.MD.3	3. 2.NBT.2
4. 2.MD.1	5. 2.NBT.8	6. 2.NBT.5
7. 2.MD.7	8. 2.NBT.7	9. 2.MD.3
10. 2.MD.8	11. 2.OA.3	12. 2.OA.2
13. 2.NBT.3	14. 2.MD.3	15. 2.OA.1

Lesson #76

1. What number does the symbol stand for? ☽ − 8 = 12

2. Write your answers in inches.
   - How long is line M?
   - How long is line N?
   - How much shorter is line N than line M?
   - What is the sum of the two lengths?

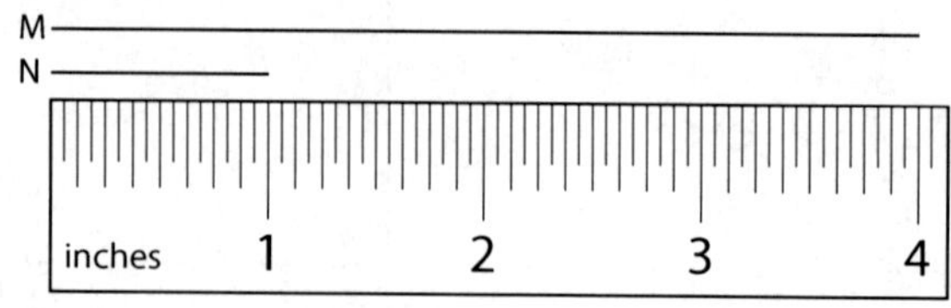

3. How much money is ten nickels?

4. What part of the circle is shaded?

5. Write forty-eight as a base-ten number.

6. Write the name of the shape that has three sides and three angles.

7. 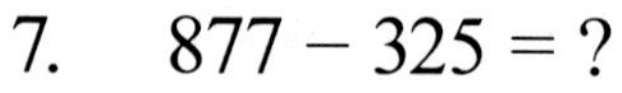 877 − 325 = ?

8. What time is it?

9. 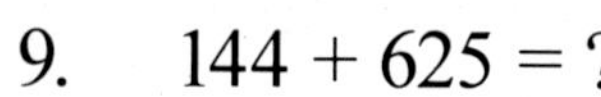 144 + 625 = ?

10. Would the young horse grow to be almost 2 centimeters or 2 meters tall?

11. Find Pencil M on page 153 of your Hands-On pages. Measure the length to the nearest centimeter.

12. Fill in the sign to make this sentence true. 703 ◯ 713

13. You would use a tape measure to find ______.
    A) how heavy a dog is
    B) how much food a dog eats
    C) how tall a dog is
    D) how loud a dog can bark

14. The graph shows items that were sold at the Bake Sale. Which item sold the most?

15. How many more pies than cakes were sold? Write a number sentence.

1. 2.OA.1	2. 2.MD.4	3. 2.MD.8
4. 2.G.3	5. 2.NBT.3	6. 2.G.1
7. 2.NBT.7	8. 2.MD.7	9. 2.NBT.7
10. 2.MD.3	11. 2.MD.3	12. 2.NBT.4
13. 2.MD.1	14. 2.MD.10	15. 2.MD.10

Lesson #77

1. What number comes just before 400?

2. Find the frog on page 152 of your Hands-On pages. Measure its length to the nearest inch.

3. 531 − 120 = ?

4. A stalactite hangs from the ceiling of a cave and grows very slowly over time. A stalactite was 3 meters long the first time it was measured. Thirty years later, the same stalactite was 7 meters long. How many meters did the stalactite grow? Write a number sentence and solve it.

   _____ + _____ = ◯

5. If you have 5 dimes and 4 pennies, how much money do you have?

6. 8 + 8 = ?

7. What is the time?

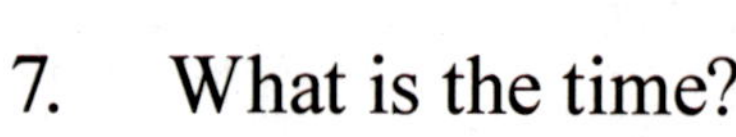

8. \$14.27 + \$13.20 = ?

9. Write the number using base-ten numerals. 80 + 900 + 4

10. Fill in the sign to make this sentence true. 503 ◯ 56

11. Could the garden hose be stretched out to almost 15 meters or 15 centimeters long?

12. Is the number of crowns even or odd? Count by 2s.

13. Count by tens. 70, 80, _____, _____, 110, 120, _____

14. Joel had 30 pieces of candy. If he gives 23 pieces to his friends, how many pieces of candy will Joel have left?

15. In which two rectangles are equal amounts shaded? Draw them.

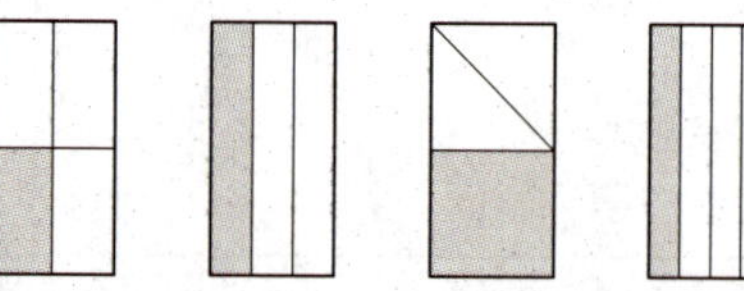

1. 2.NBT.2	2. 2.MD.3	3. 2.NBT.7
4. 2.MD.5	5. 2.MD.8	6. 2.OA.2
7. 2.MD.7	8. 2.MD.8	9. 2.NBT.3
10. 2.NBT.4	11. 2.MD.3	12. 2.OA.3
13. 2.NBT.2	14. 2.OA.1	15. 2.G.3

Lesson #78

1. The answer to what type of problem is called the sum?

2. 32 + 15 + 10 = ?

3. There were one hundred thirty-three birds in the tree. Sixty-seven of them flew away. How many birds are still in the tree?

4. Write this as a base-ten number. One hundred fifty-eight.

5. Nine quarters is the same as _____.

   $1 and 50¢ $9 $2 and 25¢ $25

6. 730 − 310 = ?

7. Write the time shown on the clock.

8. Which is longer, 7 inches or 7 feet?

9. **Ten hundred can also be read as one thousand.** Write 1,000 in the box.

10. Fill in the missing numbers. 600, 700, _____, _____, _____

11. Which circle is divided into three equal thirds? Draw it.

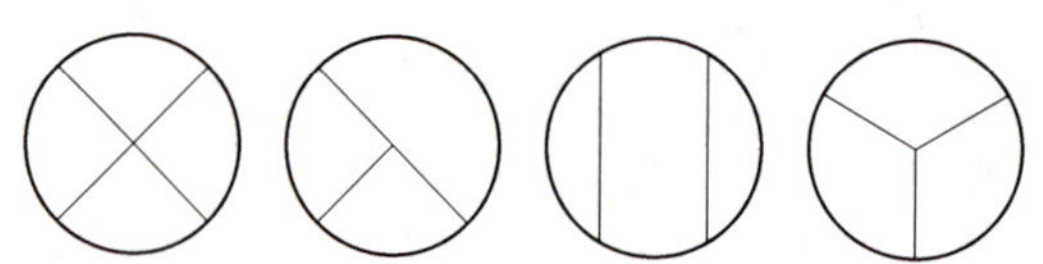

12. Find Pencil M on page 153 of your Hands-On pages. Measure the length to the nearest inch.

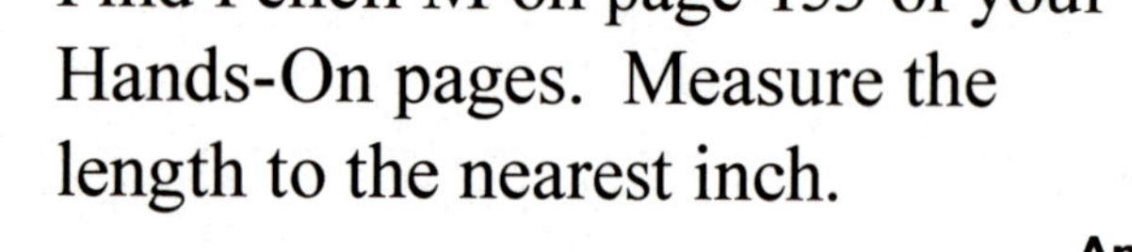

13. 316 + 312 = ?

14. How many more books did Ricardo read than Josh?

15. In all, how many books did the children read?

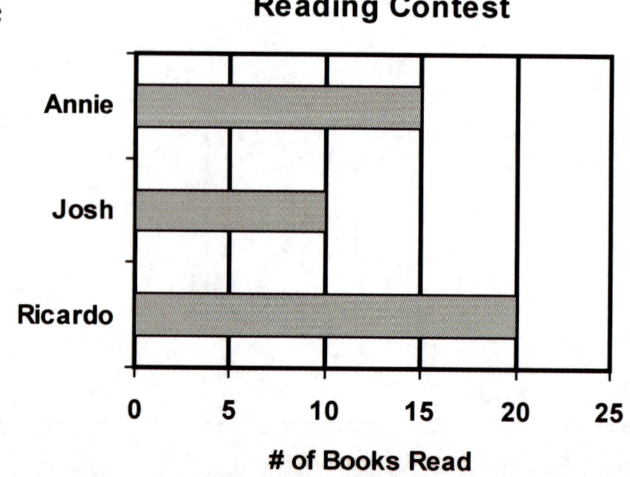

1. 1.OA.7	2. 2.NBT.6	3. 2.OA.1
4. 2.NBT.3	5. 2.MD.8	6. 2.NBT.7
7. 2.MD.7	8. 2.MD.3	9. 2.NBT.1
10. 2.NBT.2	11. 2.G.3	12. 2.MD.3
13. 2.NBT.7	14. 2.MD.10	15. 2.MD.10

Lesson #79

1. Find the ladybug on page 152 of your Hands-On pages. Measure its length to the nearest inch.

2. The picture shows how tall the plant was last week. Now, the plant is 12 inches tall. How many inches did the plant grow? Write a number sentence.

   _____ + _____ = 12

3. What time is it?

4. 117 + 662 = ?

5. Fill in the sign to make this sentence true. 516 ○ 332

6. Write your answers in centimeters.

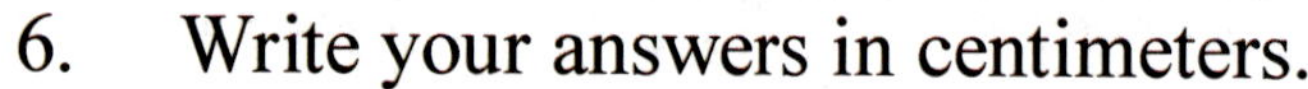

- How long is A?
- How long is B?

- How much shorter is B than A?

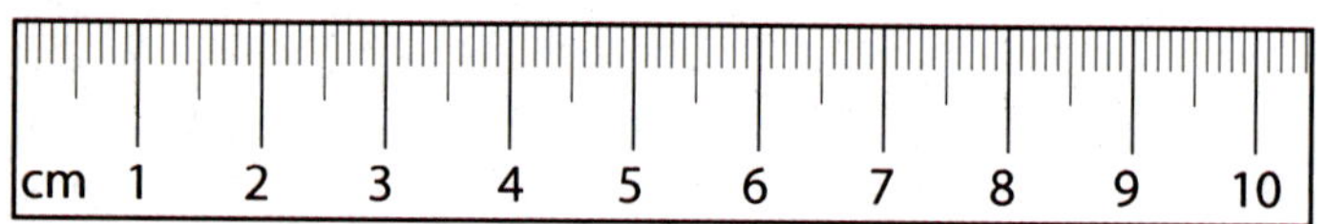

- What is the sum of the two lengths?

7. Write the missing numbers. 130, 140, ____, 160, ____, 180

8. 88 − 59 = ?

9. Is 16 closer to 10 or 20?

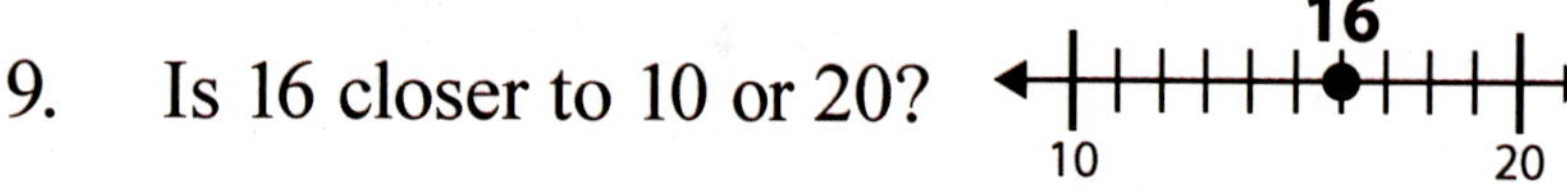

10. 5 + 6 = ?

11. Which shape is divided exactly in half? Draw it in the box.

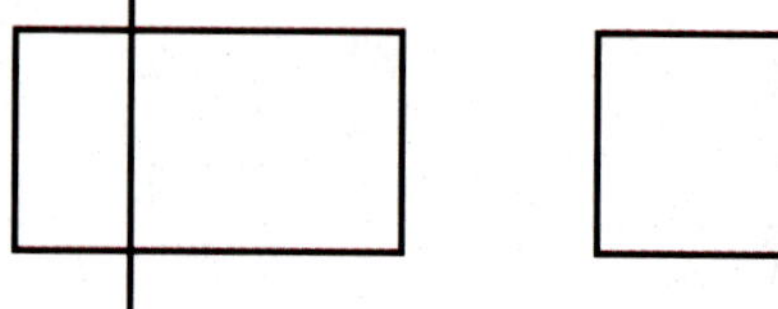

12. What number is 100 less than 278?

13. Write 242 using words.

14. If you have two dimes, six nickels and one penny, how many cents do you have?

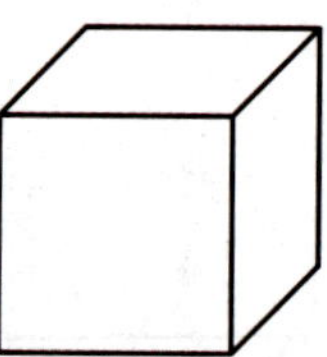

15. What is the name of this shape? How many faces does it have?

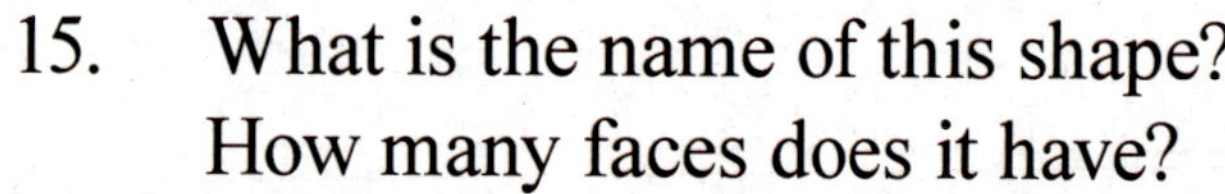

1. 2.MD.3	2. 2.MD.5	3. 2.MD.7
4. 2.NBT.7	5. 2.NBT.4	6. 2.MD.4
7. 2.NBT.2	8. 2.NBT.5	9. 3.NBT.1 (Prep)
10. 2.OA.2	11. 2.G.3	12. 2.NBT.8
13. 2.NBT.3	14. 2.MD.8	15. 2.G.1

Lesson #80

1. Draw a rectangle in your answer box. Divide the rectangle into thirds. Color a third of the rectangle.

2. Write the time.

3. 36 + 59 = ?

4. Is the number of pretzels even or odd? Count by 2s.

5. Write this number as a base-ten numeral. 6 + 100 + 20.

6. Fill in the sign to make this sentence true. 53 ◯ 56

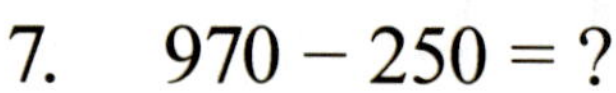

7. 970 − 250 = ?

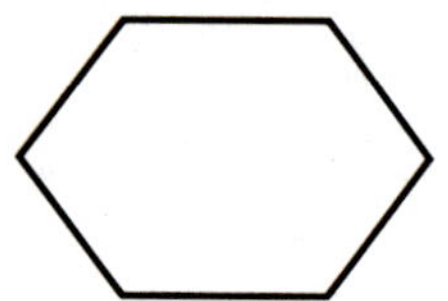

8. Name the shape.

9. 27 + 31 + 15 + 10 = ?

10. Rachel cut three pieces of celery. Each piece was 5 inches long. How many inches of celery did Rachel have? Write a number sentence and solve it.

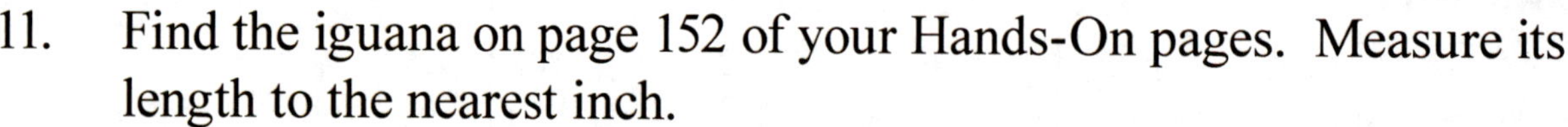

11. Find the iguana on page 152 of your Hands-On pages. Measure its length to the nearest inch.

12. Sue ate her lunch at 1:00 a.m. or 1:00 p.m.?

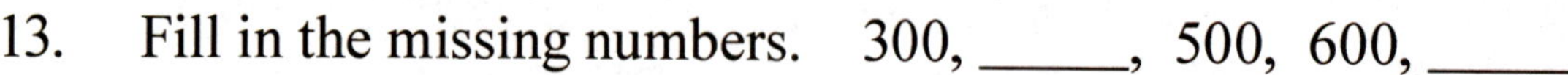

13. Fill in the missing numbers. 300, _____, 500, 600, _____

14. Which tool would you use to find the width of a refrigerator?

compass   scale   tape measure

15. What is the answer to a subtraction problem called?

1. 2.G.3	2. 2.MD.7	3. 2.NBT.5
4. 2.OA.3	5. 2.NBT.3	6. 2.NBT.4
7. 2.NBT.7	8. 2.G.1	9. 2.NBT.6
10. 2.MD.5	11. 2.MD.3	12. 2.MD.7
13. 2.NBT.2	14. 2.MD.1	15. 1.OA.7

Lesson #81

1. Fill in the sign to make this sentence true. 219 ◯ 192

2. Is 52 closer to 50 or 60?

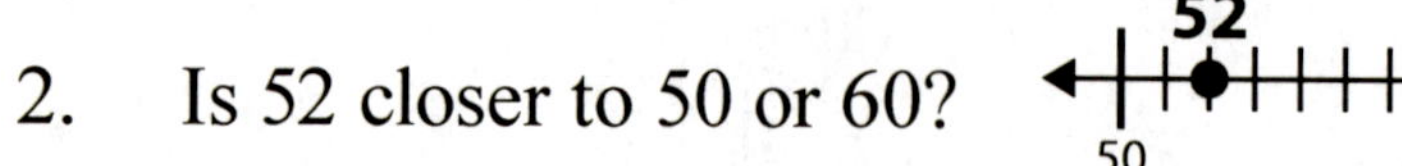

3. Would you use a tape measure or a compass to find out how many feet long a basketball court is?

4. 19 + 29 + 35 = ?

5. What time is it?

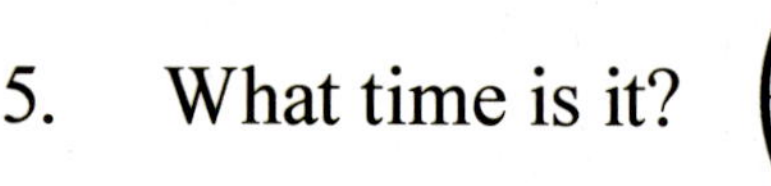

6. \$33.12 – \$15.10 = ?

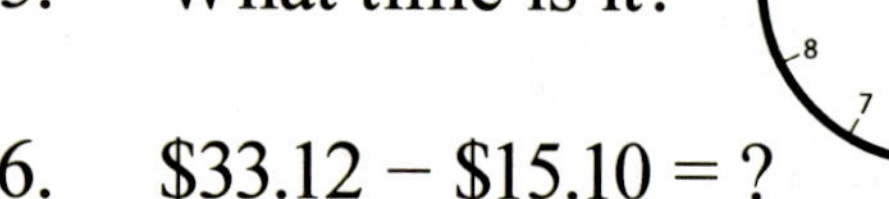

7. What base-ten number is this? 200 + 50 + 8

8. Write your answers in inches.

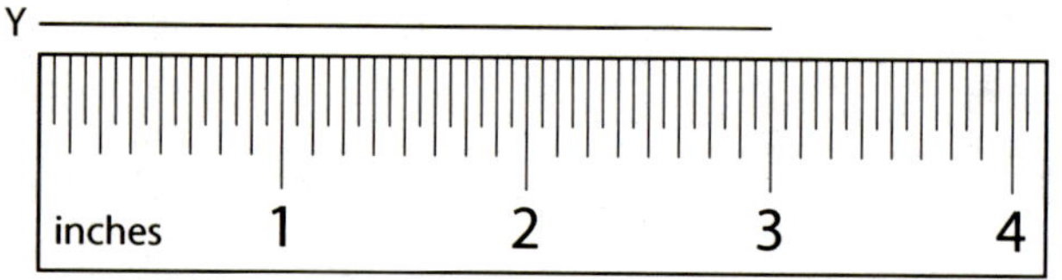

- How long is line X?
- How long is line Y?
- How much longer is line Y than line X?
- What is the sum of the two lengths?

9. Find Pencil C on page 153 of your Hands-On pages. Measure its length to the nearest inch.

10. Mentally add 100. 363, 463, _____, _____, _____, 863

11. 735 + 153 = ?

12. The same amount is shaded in which two rectangles? Draw them.

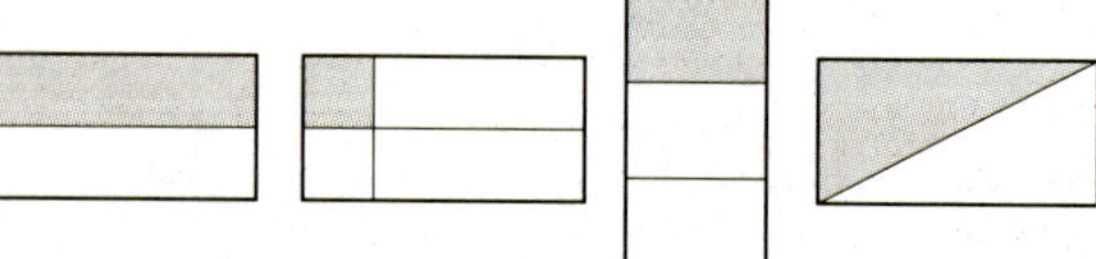

13. Which is greater, 8 quarters or \$1.00?

14. What number does the symbol stand for? ◆ + 9 = 20

15. At the zoo, the fourth graders saw 16 sharks and 8 whales. How many sharks and whales did they see altogether?

1. 2.NBT.4	2. 3.NBT.1 (Prep)	3. 2.MD.1
4. 2.NBT.6	5. 2.MD.7	6. 2.MD.8
7. 2.NBT.3	8. 2.MD.4	9. 2.MD.3
10. 2.NBT.8	11. 2.NBT.7	12. 2.G.3
13. 2.MD.8	14. 2.OA.1	15. 2.OA.1

Lesson #82

1. Count by tens. 65, 75, _____, ______

2. What is the time shown on the clock?

3. How much money is 2 quarters and 3 dimes?

4. What number does the symbol stand for? ✿ – 12 = 20

5. 575 – 255 = ?

6. Is 93 closer to 90 or 100?

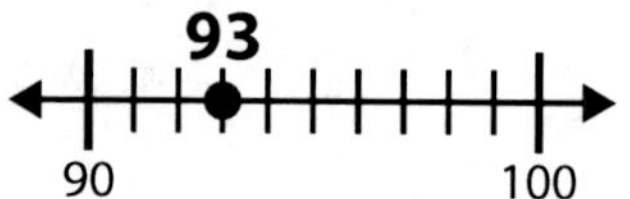

7. 27 + 52 + 19 = ?

8. Which rectangles are divided into three thirds? Draw them.

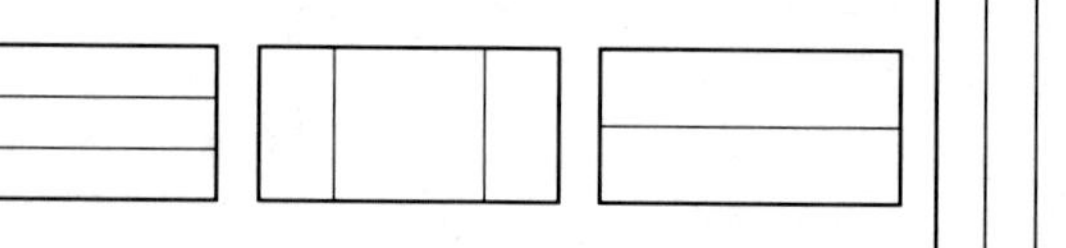

9. Is a Ferris wheel almost 40 centimeters or 40 meters high?

10. What is the name of the shape?

cone　　cylinder　　cube

11. Write this as a base-ten numeral. 3 hundreds, 7 tens, and 9 ones

12. Find the worm on page 152 of your Hands-On pages. Measure its length to the nearest centimeter.

13. Shawna's number is five less than 30. What is Shawna's number?

14. Which tools can you use to find out how long or wide something is? Write the words in your answer box.

clock	ruler	yardstick
meter stick	tape measure	test tube

15. Which two holidays equal 25 votes?

How many more students chose Halloween than chose Valentine's Day?

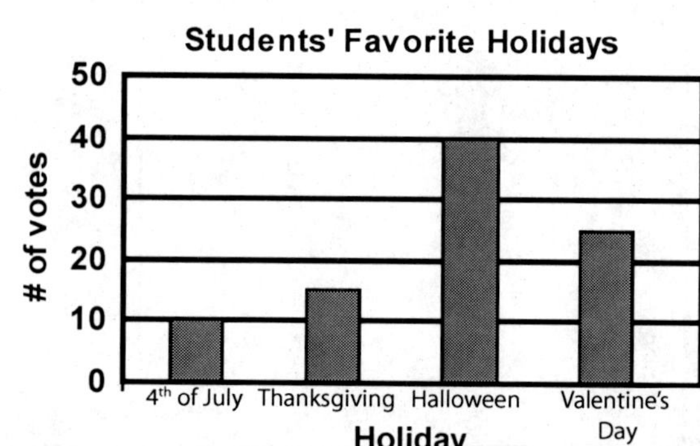

1. 2.NBT.2	2. 2.MD.7	3. 2.MD.8
4. 2.OA.1	5. 2.NBT.7	6. 3.NBT.1 (Prep)
7. 2.NBT.6	8. 2.G.3	9. 2.MD.3
10. 1.G.2	11. 2.NBT.3	12. 2.MD.3
13. 2.NBT.8	14. 2.MD.1	15. 2.MD.10

Lesson #83

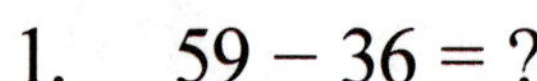

1. 59 − 36 = ?

2. Is 88 closer to 80 or 90?

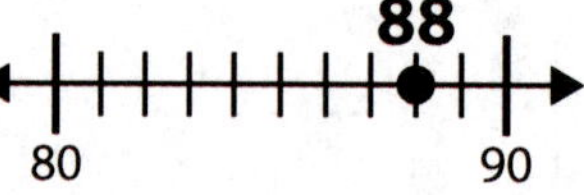

3. The sum is the answer to a(n) ___________ problem.

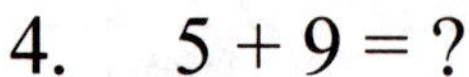

4. 5 + 9 = ?

5. Write the time shown on the clock.

6. Write 639 using words.

7. Fill in the sign to make this sentence true. 98 ◯ 135

8. Jeremy rode 24 miles on Friday. He rode 18 miles on Saturday and 32 miles on Sunday. How many miles did he ride in all?

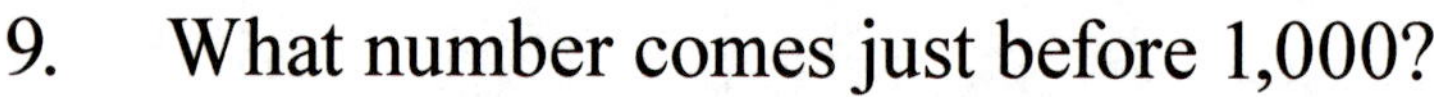

9. What number comes just before 1,000?

10. Find the frog on page 152 of your Hands-On pages. Measure its length to the nearest centimeter.

11. 743 + 144 = ?

12. There were 45 popsicles in the freezer. After Lyndie and her friends ate some popsicles, there were 40. How many popsicles did Lyndie and her friends eat? Finish the number sentence. First write the minus sign, and then fill in the blank.

45 ◯ ______ = 40

13. Mentally add 100. 413, 513, _____, _____, 813

14. 19 + 26 + 41 + 12 = ?

15. How much of each rectangle is shaded?

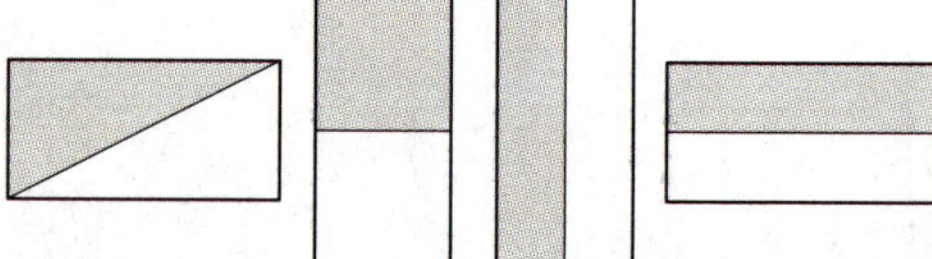

1. 2.NBT.5	2. 3.NBT.1 (Prep)	3. 1.OA.7
4. 2.OA.2	5. 2.MD.7	6. 2.NBT.3
7. 2.NBT.4	8. 2.MD.5	9. 2.NBT.2
10. 2.MD.3	11. 2.NBT.7	12. 2.OA.1
13. 2.NBT.8	14. 2.NBT.6	15. 2.G.3

Lesson #84

1. What base-ten number is this? 800 + 60 + 2

2. Fill in the sign to make this sentence true. 86 ◯ 74

3. Which is the best tool for finding out how many centimeters long a bookshelf is?

   yardstick   compass   ruler   meter stick

4. An amusement park had 335 visitors on Friday and 243 visitors on Saturday. How many visitors did they have in all?

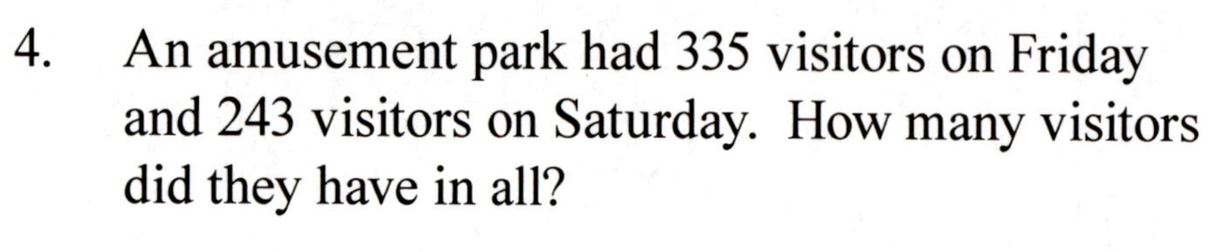

5. What number is 100 more than 150?

6. For a good fit, would John's pants be 60 centimeters or 60 meters long?

7. What is the name of this shape?

8. Write the missing numbers in the list. 130, 140, _____, 160, _____, 180

9. Which is greater, 3 quarters or 10 dimes?

10. 64 − 28 = ?

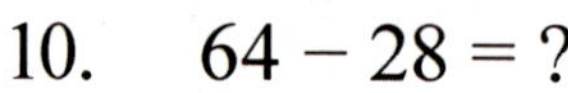

11. What time is shown?

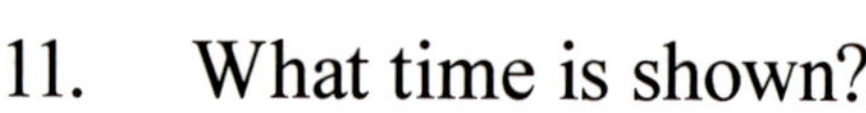

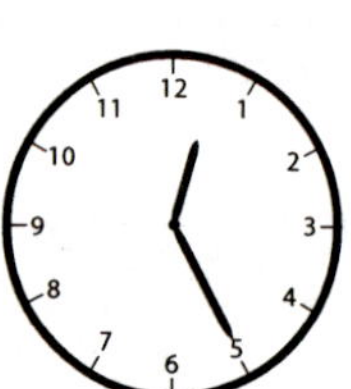

12. 317 + 332 = ?

13. Is the number of soaps even or odd? Count by 2s.

14. Which shapes are divided into four fourths? Draw them.

15. Find the snail on page 152 of your Hands-On pages. Measure its length to the nearest centimeter.

1. 2.NBT.3	2. 2.NBT.4	3. 2.MD.1
4. 2.OA.1	5. 2.NBT.8	6. 2.MD.3
7. 1.G.2	8. 2.NBT.2	9. 2.MD.8
10. 2.NBT.5	11. 2.MD.7	12. 2.NBT.7
13. 2.OA.3	14. 2.G.3	15. 2.MD.3

Lesson #85

1. Fill in the sign to make this sentence true. 806 ○ 806

2. What is the name of this shape? How many faces does it have?
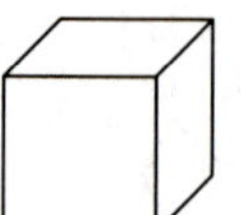

3. Nela's number is 10 less than 40. What is Nela's number?

4. Mentally add 100. 341, 441, _____, _____, _____

5. Write 724 using words.
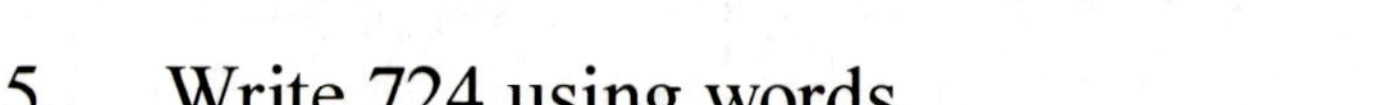

6. 536 − 234 = ?
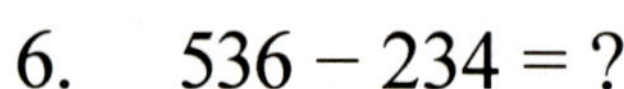

7. What time is it?

8. 98 + 64 = ?

9. \$55.35 + \$24.53 = ?

10. Which tools can you use to find out how long or wide something is? Write the words in your answer box.

yardstick	ruler	clock
meter stick	scale	air pump

11. Match the amounts that are equal.

_____	45¢	A) two quarters and a nickel
_____	55¢	B) a quarter, two dimes, and a nickel
_____	50¢	C) four dimes and five pennies

12. Would a cell phone be 4 inches or 14 inches wide?

13. Draw a rectangle in your answer box. Divide the rectangle into fourths. Color a fourth of the rectangle.
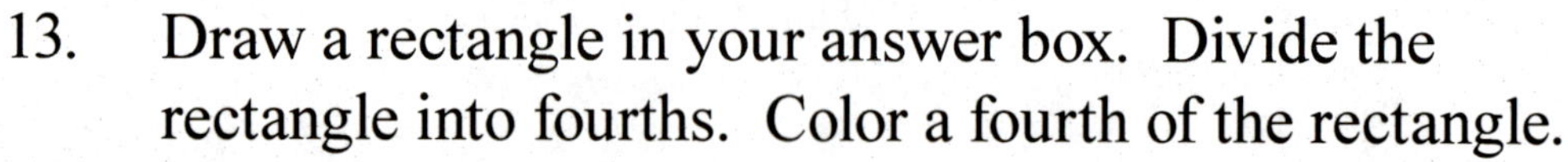

14. Find the ant on page 152 of your Hands-On pages. Measure its length to the nearest centimeter.
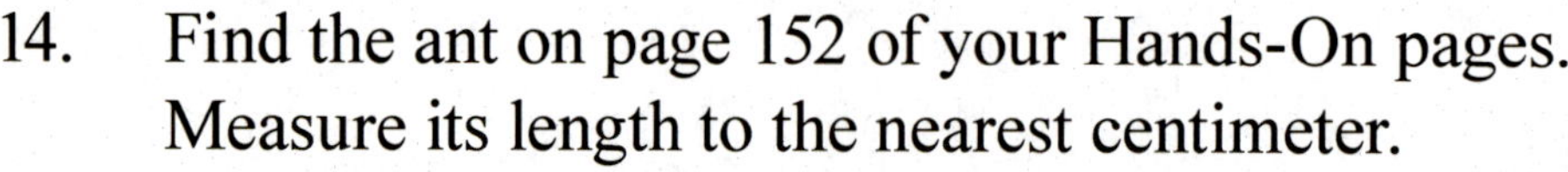

15. There are three rows in this picture. How many columns are there?
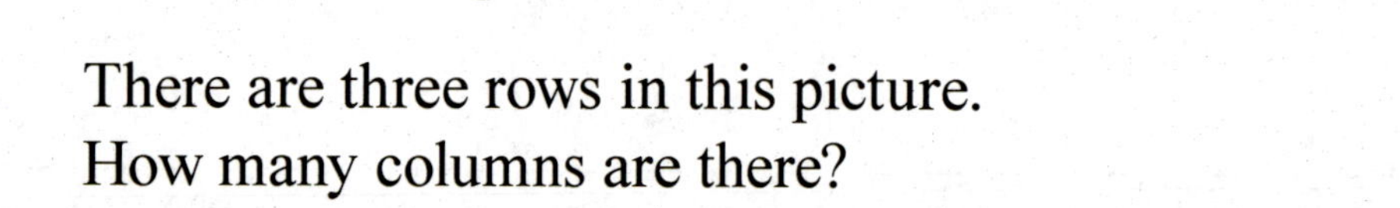

1. 2.NBT.4	2. 2.G.1	3. 2.NBT.8
4. 2.NBT.8	5. 2.NBT.3	6. 2.NBT.7
7. 2.MD.7	8. 2.NBT.5	9. 2.MD.8
10. 2.MD.1	11. 2.MD.8	12. 2.MD.3
13. 2.G.3	14. 2.MD.3	15. 2.OA.4

Lesson #86

1. Find the popsicle stick on page 152 of your Hands-On pages. Measure its length to the nearest centimeter.

2. Write the time shown on the clock.

3. Fill in the sign to make this sentence true. 842 ◯ 1,000

4. 36 + 12 + 24 = ?

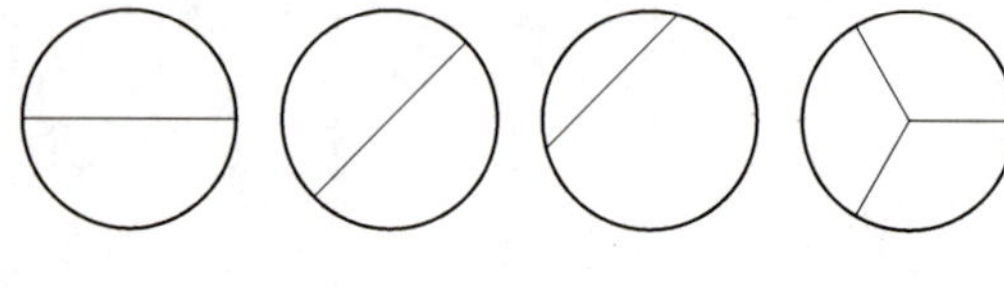

5. Which shapes are divided into two equal halves? Draw them.

6. Which is greater, 10 nickels or 4 dimes?

7. A shape with four sides and four angles is called a _____.

quadrilateral pentagon hexagon

8. Count by fives. 35, 40, ____, _____, _____

9. 695 − 272 = ?

10. I have 7 hundreds, 4 tens and 3 ones. What number am I?

11. Harry is 5 years older than Susan. Susan is 2 years younger than Nick. Nick is 10 years old. How old is Harry?

12. Is the number of bees even or odd? Count by 2s.

13. The answer to a subtraction problem is the __________.

14. There are two bookcases in Mr. Green's classroom. One bookcase is 24 inches wide. The other bookcase is 26 inches wide. Will both bookcases fit in a space that is 52 inches wide? Write a number sentence and solve it.

15. How many rows are in this picture?

1. 2.MD.3	2. 2.MD.7	3. 2.NBT.4
4. 2.NBT.6	5. 2.G.3	6. 2.MD.8
7. 2.G.1	8. 2.NBT.2	9. 2.NBT.7
10. 2.NBT.3	11. 2.OA.1	12. 2.OA.3
13. 1.OA.7	14. 2.MD.5	15. 2.OA.4

Lesson #87

1. Dad gave Sam $2.00. Sam bought a box of candy that cost $1.50. How much money does Sam have now?

2. What number does the symbol stand for?
   99 – ♥ = 93

3. Would a letter just fit in an envelope that is 20 centimeters or 20 meters long?

4. $87.75 – $32.25 = ?

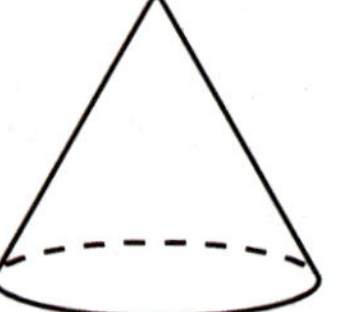

5. What is the name of the shape?

6. The answer to an addition problem is called the ___________.

7. The same amount is shaded in which two squares? Draw them.

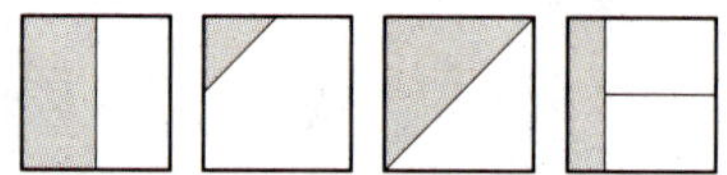

8. 336 + 253 = ?

9. What time is shown on the clock?

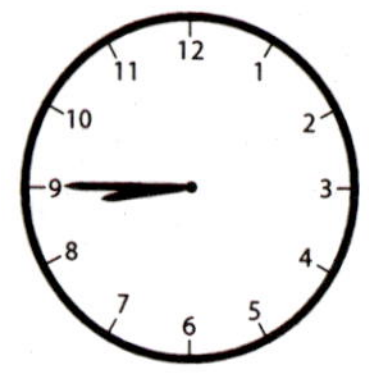

10. 90 – 47 = ?

11. Is 47 closer to 40 or 50?

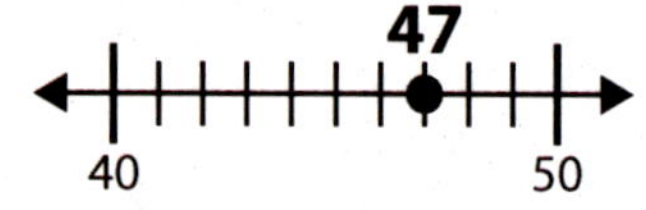

12. What number comes between 599 and 601?

13. Write this as a base-ten numeral. 500 + 2 + 30

14. 5 + 5 + 5 + 5 = ?

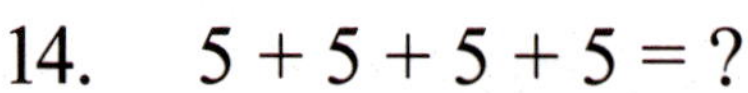

15. How many boats were on the lake in all?

    How many more motorboats than canoes were on the lake?

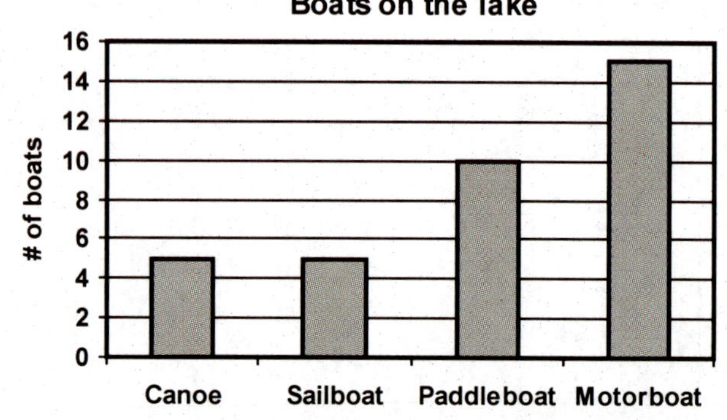

1. 2.MD.8	2. 2.OA.1	3. 2.MD.3
4. 2.MD.8	5. 1.G.2	6. 1.OA.7
7. 2.G.3	8. 2.NBT.7	9. 2.MD.7
10. 2.NBT.5	11. 3.NBT.1 (Prep)	12. 2.NBT.2
13. 2.NBT.3	14. 2.OA.2	15. 2.MD.10

Lesson #88

1. Find the egg on page 152 of your Hands-On pages. Measure its height to the nearest centimeter.

2. 9 + 8 = ?

3. Mentally add 100. 126, 226, _____, _____, 526, _____

4. If you have ten pennies, two dimes, and a quarter, how many cents do you have?

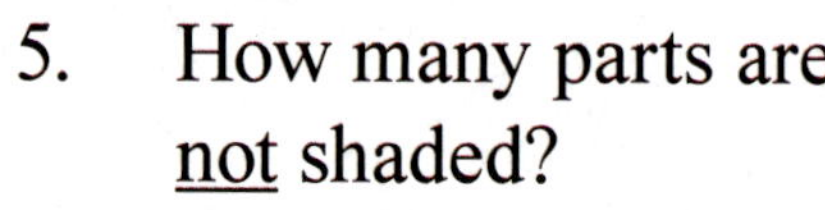

5. How many parts are not shaded?

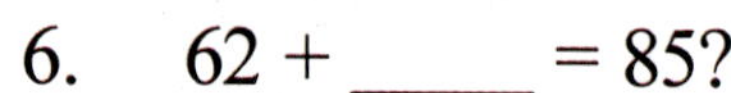

6. 62 + _____ = 85?

7. 89 − 64 = ?

8. What time is shown?

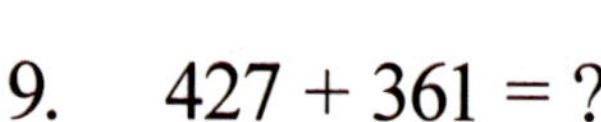

9. 427 + 361 = ?

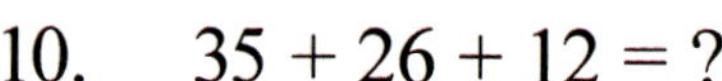

10. 35 + 26 + 12 = ?

11. What base-ten number is this? 800 + 50 + 6

12. What tool would you use to find the length of a swimming pool in inches?

    meter stick   timer   tape measure

13. Would a new model telephone be 10 meters or 10 centimeters long?

14. Write your answers in inches.

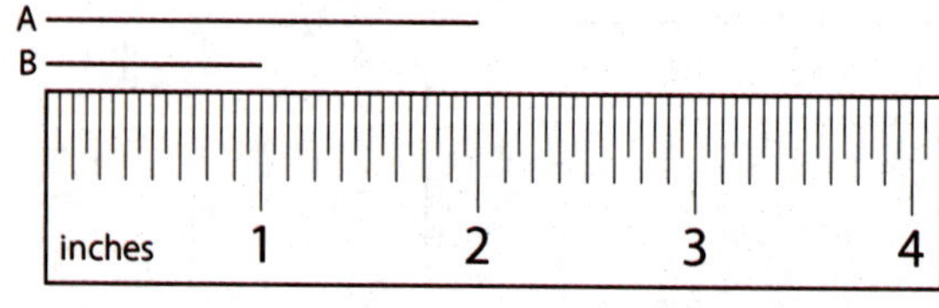

- How long is line A?
- How long is line B?
- How much shorter is line B than line A?
- What is the sum of the two lengths?

15. Amanda spent $1.25 on candy and $1.40 on a drink. How much money did she spend altogether?

1. 2.MD.3	2. 2.OA.2	3. 2.NBT.8
4. 2.MD.8	5. 2.G.3	6. 2.OA.1
7. 2.NBT.5	8. 2.MD.7	9. 2.NBT.7
10. 2.NBT.6	11. 2.NBT.3	12. 2.MD.1
13. 2.MD.3	14. 2.MD.4	15. 2.MD.8

Lesson #89

1. What number is 100 less than 763?

2. Write your answers in inches.
   - How long is screw A?
   - How long is screw B?
   - How much longer is screw A than screw B?
   - What is the sum of the two lengths?

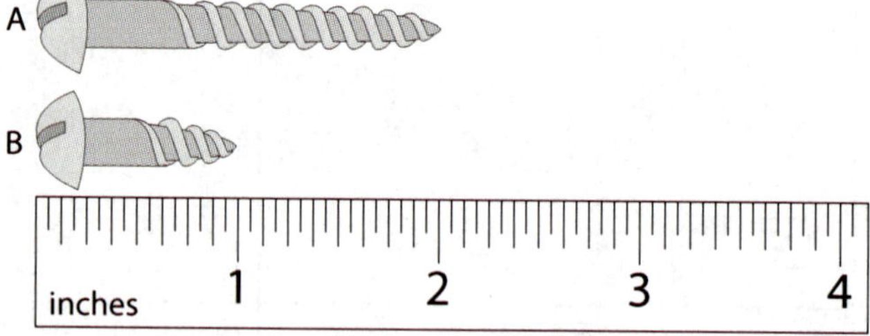

3. What number does the symbol stand for? 16 – 8 = ♠

4. Count by fives. 65, 70, _____, _____, 85, _____, _____

5. 628 – 312 = ?

6. Which shapes are divided into three equal thirds? Draw them.

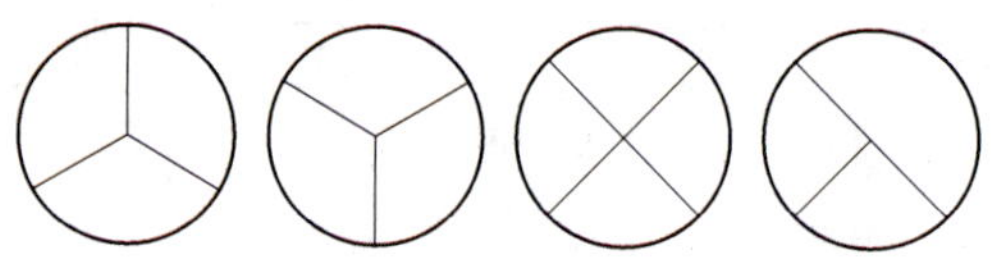

7. A park bench is 67 inches wide. A pathway is 42 inches wide. How much wider is the bench than the pathway? Write a number sentence and solve it.

8. Fill in the sign to make this sentence true. 508 ◯ 518

9. 38 + 16 + 21 = ?

10. What time is shown on the clock?

11. I have six tens and five ones. What number am I?

12. The answer to a subtraction problem is the _______.

13. Which is more money, 6 dimes or 2 quarters?

14. There are two columns. How many rows are in this picture?

15. There are 30 students in one second grade class and 26 students in the other. How many second graders are there in all?

1. 2.NBT.8	2. 2.MD.4	3. 2.OA.1
4. 2.NBT.2	5. 2.NBT.7	6. 2.G.3
7. 2.MD.5	8. 2.NBT.4	9. 2.NBT.6
10. 2.MD.7	11. 2.NBT.3	12. 1.OA.7
13. 2.MD.8	14. 2.OA.4	15. 2.OA.1

Lesson #90

1. 123 + 456 = ?

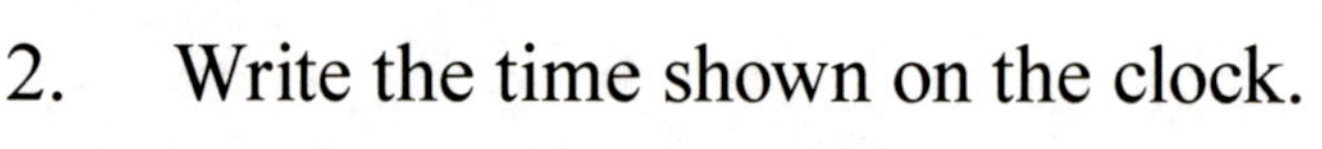

2. Write the time shown on the clock.

3. 75 − 58 = ?

4. Sal's pencil is 4 inches long, Fran's pencil is 7 inches long, and Jim's pencil is 6 inches long. If the three students laid the pencils from end to end, how long would the line of pencils be? Write a number sentence.

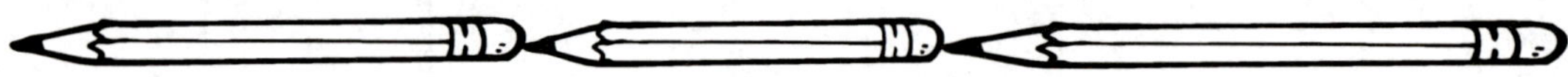

5. The number 400 has ____ hundreds, _____ tens, and _____ ones.

6. Give the name of each shape.

A) 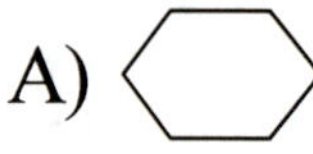 B)  C) 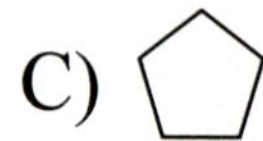

7. Is 43 closer to 40 or 50?

43
40 50

8. 25 + 25 + 25 + 15 = ?

9. If you have ten dimes, and two nickels, do you have more or less than a dollar?

10. Which shapes are divided into four fourths? Draw them.

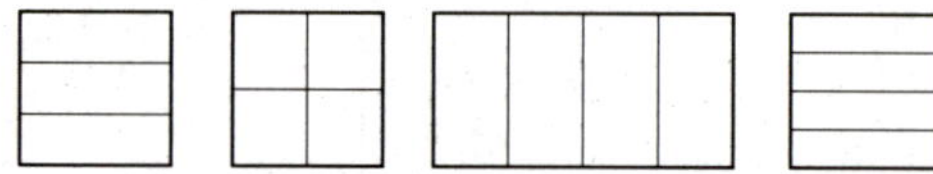

11. Find the nail on page 152 of your Hands-On pages. Measure its length to the nearest centimeter.

12. Is the number of cats even or odd? Count by 2s.

13. Carol had eight jars. She put two marbles in each jar. How many marbles were there altogether? (Draw a picture to help you.)

14. What number comes just before 1,000?

15. How many columns are in this picture?

1. 2.NBT.7	2. 2.MD.7	3. 2.NBT.5
4. 2.MD.5	5. 2.NBT.1	6. 2.G.1, 1.G.2
7. 3.NBT.1 (Prep)	8. 2.NBT.6	9. 2.MD.8
10. 2.G.3	11. 2.MD.3	12. 2.OA.3
13. 2.OA.1	14. 2.NBT.2	15. 2.OA.4

Lesson #91

1. Write this number using base-ten numerals. 8 + 10 + 600

2. What tool would you use to find out how many feet long a sliding board is?

   scale   tape measure   meter stick

3. Dave and Cindy began collecting seashells on Friday. They collected 80 shells by Saturday. By Sunday, the children had collected 88 shells in all. How many seashells did Dave and Cindy collect on Sunday?

4. What number is 100 more than 750?

5. Would the public swimming pool be 25 centimeters or 25 meters wide?

6. 556 + 233 = ?

7. 32 + 37 + 25 = ?

8. 93 − 48 = ?

9. Which is longer, 4 inches or 4 feet?

10. Which shapes are divided into four fourths? Draw them.

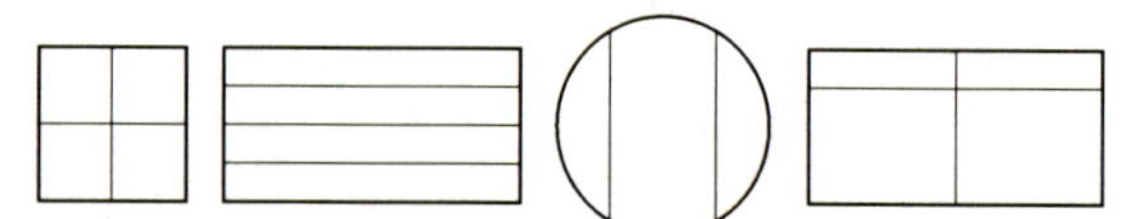

11. Draw two different quadrilaterals and name them.

12 – 15. Use the information in the chart to make a picture graph. (See *Help Pages*.)

- Give the graph a title.
- Write a label on each line. (One on the left and one on the bottom.)
- Fill in the key. Show 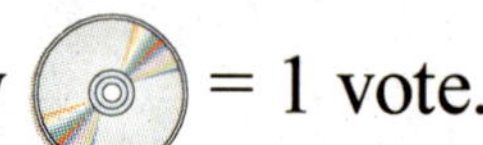 = 1 vote.
- Draw the correct number of CDs next to each type of music.

Music	# of Votes
Pop	2
Hip Hop	5
R & B	3

1. 2.NBT.3	2. 2.MD.1	3. 2.OA.1
4. 2.NBT.8	5. 2.MD.3	6. 2.NBT.7
7. 2.NBT.6	8. 2.NBT.5	9. 2.MD.3
10. 2.G.3	12 – 15. 2.MD.10	
11. 2.G.1		

Pop	
Hip Hop	
R & B	

Key:

Lesson #92

1. Write the base-ten number for seven hundred fifty-two.

2. 364 ◯ 463

3. What tool would you use to find the width of a football field in meters?

   meter stick yard stick clock

4. Which is more money, $2.00 or 7 quarters?

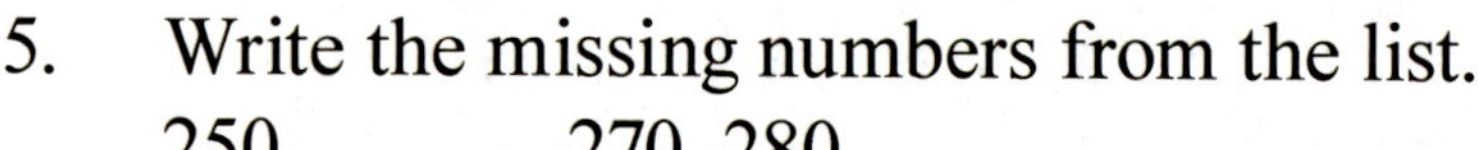

5. Write the missing numbers from the list.
   250, _____, 270, 280, _____

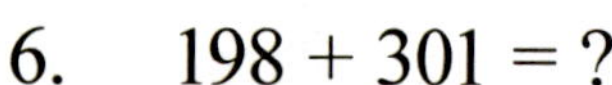

6. 198 + 301 = ?

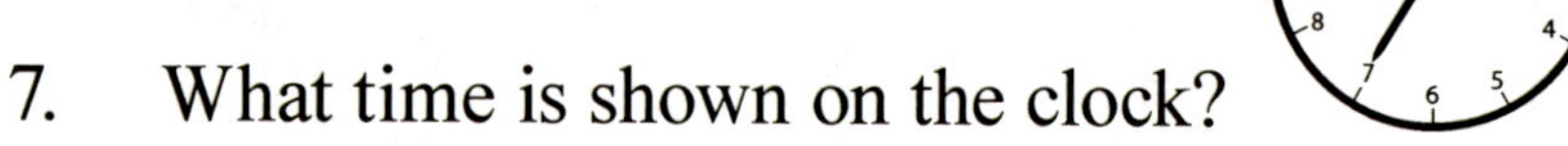

7. What time is shown on the clock?

8. 32 + 14 + 45 = ?

9. 24 − 8 = ?

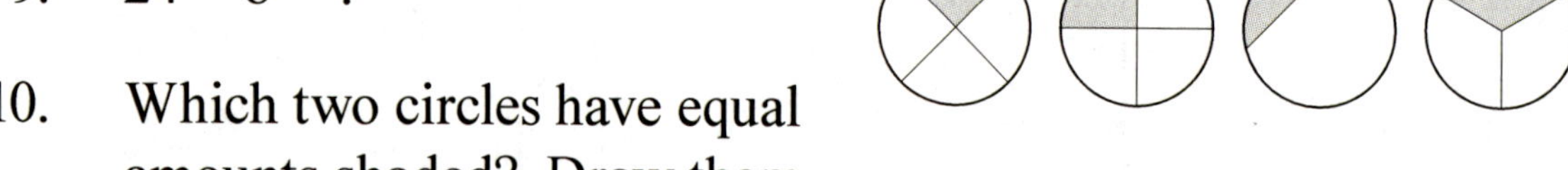

10. Which two circles have equal amounts shaded? Draw them.

11. Annie buys a pack of laces for her rollerblades that cost 56¢. She buys socks for $1.50. How much did she spend in all?

12. **A round, solid shape is called a *sphere*.** 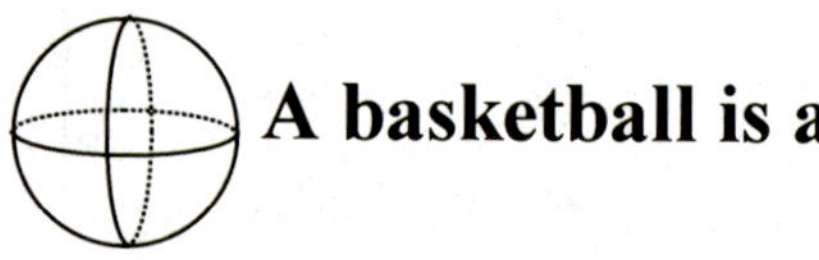 **A basketball is a sphere.** Write sphere in the box.

13. The answer to a(n) __________ problem is the difference.

14. Would Eli's new colored pencils be 17 meters or 17 centimeters long?

15. This array has three rows and four columns. Write a number sentence with three addends to show how many bears there are.

_____ + _____ + _____ = 12

1. 2.NBT.3	2. 2.NBT.4	3. 2.MD.1
4. 2.MD.8	5. 2.NBT.2	6. 2.NBT.7
7. 2.MD.7	8. 2.NBT.6	9. 2.NBT.5
10. 2.G.3	11. 2.MD.8	12. 1.G.2
13. 1.OA.7	14. 2.MD.3	15. 2.OA.4

Lesson #93

1. Write this number using base-ten numerals. Five hundred sixty-one

2. **The sum of two equal addends is an even number.** Write the sums.

   3 + 3 = _____ 6 is an even number.

   7 + 7 = _____ 14 is an even number.

   6 + 6 = _____ 12 is an even number.

3. 72 − 49 = ?

4. Find the stick on page 152 of your Hands-On pages. Measure its length to the nearest centimeter.

5. Would you use a meter stick to find the length of a cell phone in inches?

6. Would the window in Mrs. White's kitchen be 2 centimeters or 2 meters tall?

7. 26 + 9 + 31 = ?

8. Len's number is 20 less than 100. What is Len's number?

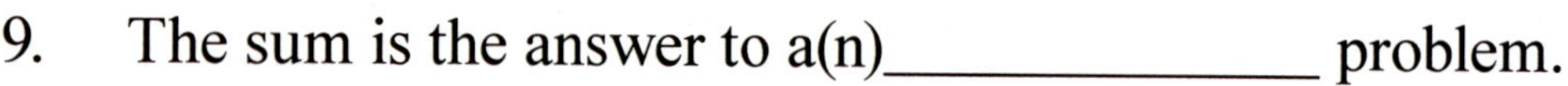

9. The sum is the answer to a(n)______________ problem.

10. Fill in the sign to make this sentence true. 89 ◯ 96

11. Count the objects in the array. Write an addition sentence to show the sum.

_____ + _____ = _____

12. Fill in the missing number. 18 + _____ = 26

13. Is a swing set about 6 feet tall or 6 inches tall?

14. 516 + 273 = ?

15. How many more cans than bottles were collected?

    How many items were collected altogether?

Recycling	
Item	**# Collected**
Bottles	12
Cans	34
Papers	45

1. 2.NBT.3	2. 2.OA.3	3. 2.NBT.5
4. 2.MD.3	5. 2.MD.1	6. 2.MD.3
7. 2.NBT.5	8. 2.OA.1	9. 1.OA.7
10. 2.NBT.4	11. 2.OA.4	12. 2.OA.1
13. 2.MD.3	14. 2.NBT.7	15. 2.MD.10

Lesson #94

1. How many cents do you have if you have two quarters, two nickels and seven pennies?

2. Is 18 closer to ten or twenty?

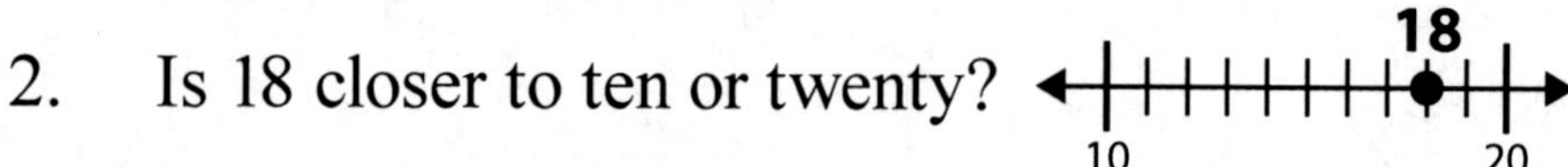

3. 63 + 28 = ?

4. What is the name of the shape?

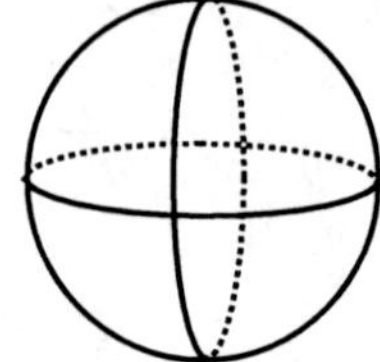

cube   cylinder   sphere

5. In an aquarium there are 16 goldfish, 10 angelfish and 4 clownfish. How many fish are in the aquarium?

6. What number does the symbol stand for? 9 + ☽ = 18

7. Find the ladybug on page 152 of your Hands-On pages. Measure its length to the nearest centimeter.

8. The sum is the answer to a(n) ______________ problem.

9. Which shapes are divided into four fourths? Draw them.

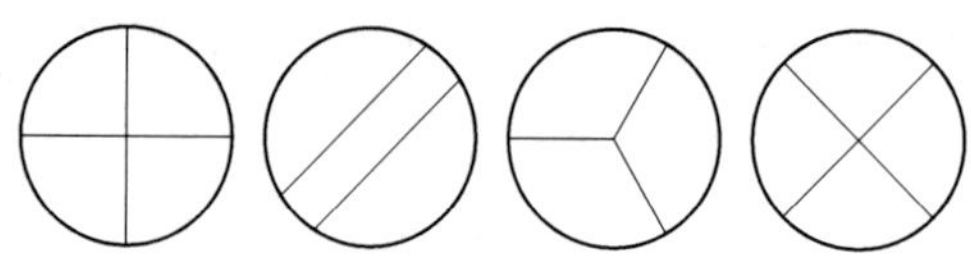

10. 92 − 63 = ?

11. Write your answers in inches.
    - How long is screw A?
    - How long is screw B?
    - How much shorter is screw A than screw B?
    - What is the sum of the two lengths?

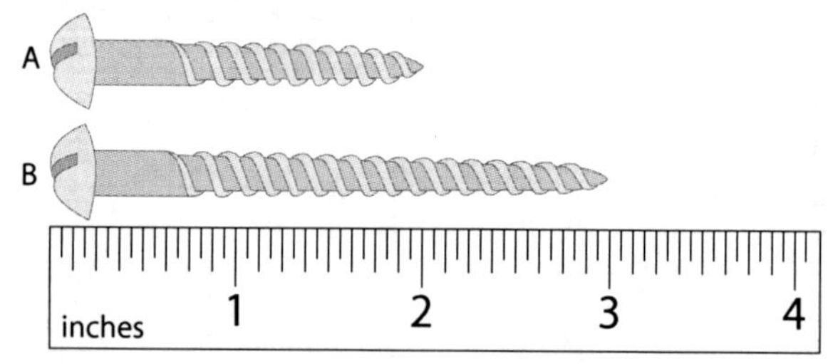

12. Write the number using base-ten numerals. 29 tens

13. Would you use a yard stick to find the width of a movie screen in meters?

14. Would the red caboose be 10 meters or 10 centimeters long?

15. The sum of two equal addends is an even number. Write the sums.

4 + 4 = _____
8 is an even number.

5 + 5 = _____
10 is an even number.

2 + 2 = _____
4 is an even number.

1. 2.MD.8	2. 3.NBT.1 (Prep)	3. 2.NBT.5
4. 1.G.2	5. 2.OA.1	6. 2.OA.1
7. 2.MD.3	8. 1.OA.7	9. 2.G.3
10. 2.NBT.5	11. 2.MD.4	12. 2.NBT.3
13. 2.MD.1	14. 2.MD.3	15. 2.OA.3

Lesson #95

1. Would you use a compass or a tape measure to find out how many feet long a tree branch is?

2. Write the name of the shape.

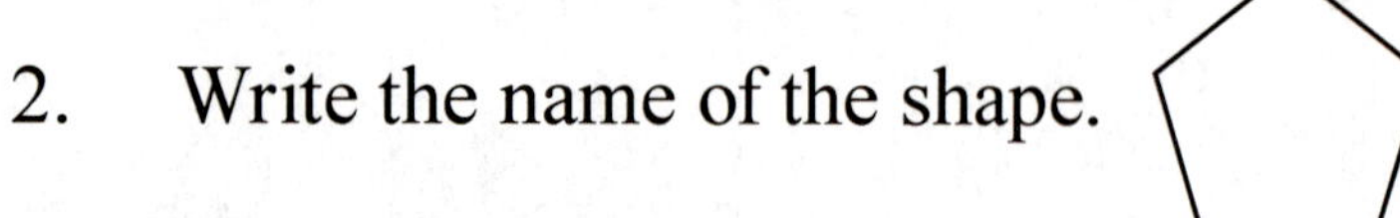

3. 50¢ − 15¢ = ?

4. Count the objects in the array. Write an addition sentence to show the sum.

_____ + _____ = _____

5. Would an old oak tree be 2 meters or 18 meters tall?

6. There were 38 poodles in the dog show. If twelve poodles drop out of the show, how many poodles are left?

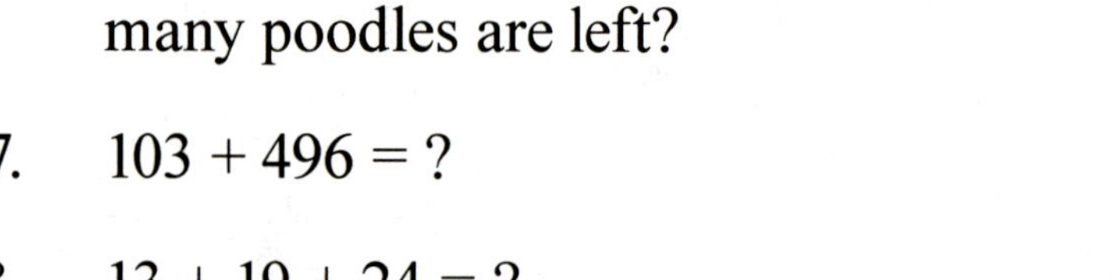

7. 103 + 496 = ?

8. 13 + 19 + 24 = ?

9. Write the number using base-ten numerals. 41 tens

10. Which shapes are divided into two equal halves? Draw them.

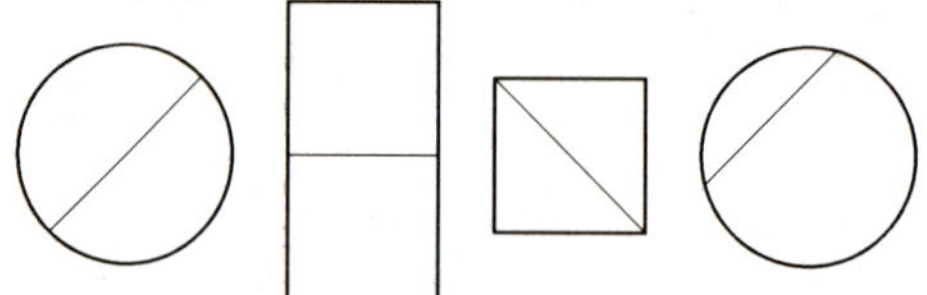

11. Jerry grew 6 centimeters last year. His brother grew 5 centimeters and his sister grew 4 centimeters. How many centimeters did the children grow all together? Write a number sentence to find the answer.

12. What number does the symbol stand for? ★ − 12 = 8

13. Find the credit card on page 152 of your Hands-On pages. Measure its length to the nearest centimeter.

14. Count by 100s. 300, 400, _____, _____, 700, _____, _____

15. What base-ten number is this? 100 + 60 + 4

1. 2.MD.1	2. 2.G.1	3. 2.MD.8
4. 2.OA.4	5. 2.MD.3	6. 2.OA.1
7. 2.NBT.7	8. 2.NBT.6	9. 2.NBT.3
10. 2.G.3	11. 2.MD.5	12. 2.OA.1
13. 2.MD.3	14. 2.NBT.2	15. 2.NBT.3

Lesson #96

1. Write this number using base-ten numerals. 77 tens

2. Would you use a meter stick or yardstick to find out how many centimeters wide a picture frame is?

3. What time is shown on the clock?

4. 508 + 151 = ?

5. Fill in the sign to make this sentence true. 25 ○ 25 = 50

6. Can a polar bear grow to almost 7 feet or 70 feet high?

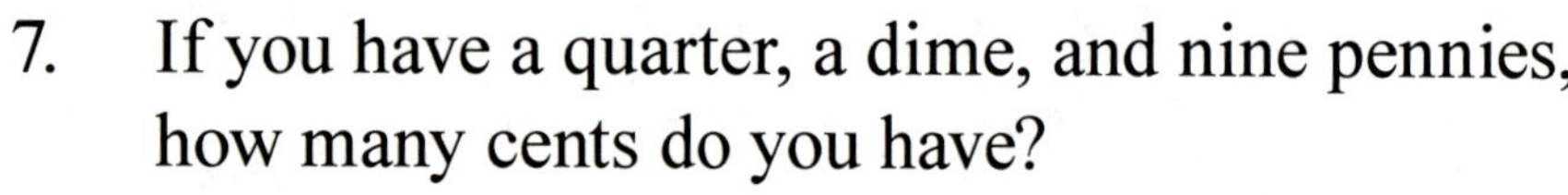

7. If you have a quarter, a dime, and nine pennies, how many cents do you have?

8. What number is 100 more than 250?

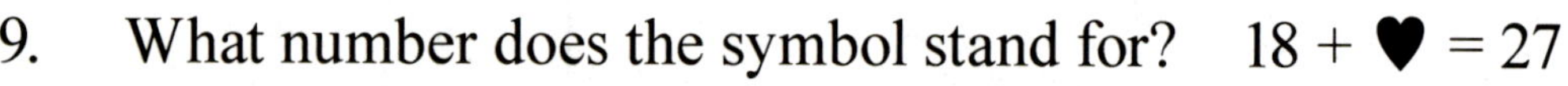

9. What number does the symbol stand for? 18 + ♥ = 27

10. Count by tens. 110, 120, _____, _____, 150, _____

11. 4 + 9 is the same as ____ + 5. Both are equal to 13.

12 – 15. Use the information (data) in the chart to make a bar graph. (See *Help Pages*.)

- Give the graph a title.
- Write a label on each line (one on the left and one at the bottom).
- Fill in the numbers for the left side of the graph. Zero is given. Go up by 1s.
- Color or shade in each bar to a height on the graph that matches the number on the chart.

Music	# of Votes
Pop	4
Country	3
Latin	6

1. 2.NBT.3	2. 2.MD.1	3. 2.MD.7
4. 2.NBT.7	5. 2.NBT.4	6. 2.MD.3
7. 2.MD.8	8. 2.NBT.8	9. 2.OA.1
10. 2.NBT.2	12 – 15. 2.MD.10	
11. 2.OA.2		

0

Lesson #97

1. Mia has \$1.50. Does she have enough money to buy a pen for 60¢ and a notebook for 95¢?

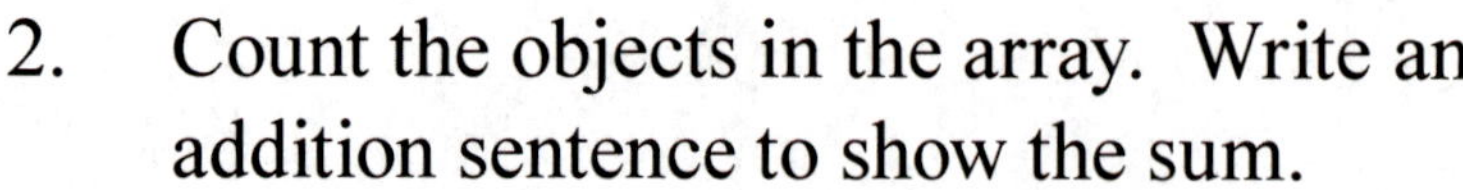

2. Count the objects in the array. Write an addition sentence to show the sum.

_____ + _____ + _____ = _____

3. 333 + 466 = ?

4. The answer to a subtraction problem is the ________.

5. Write your answers in inches.

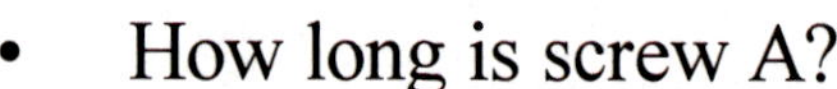

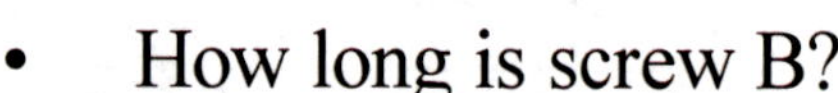

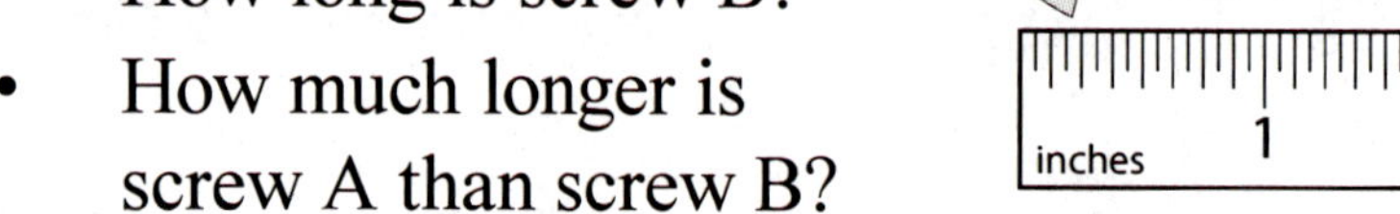

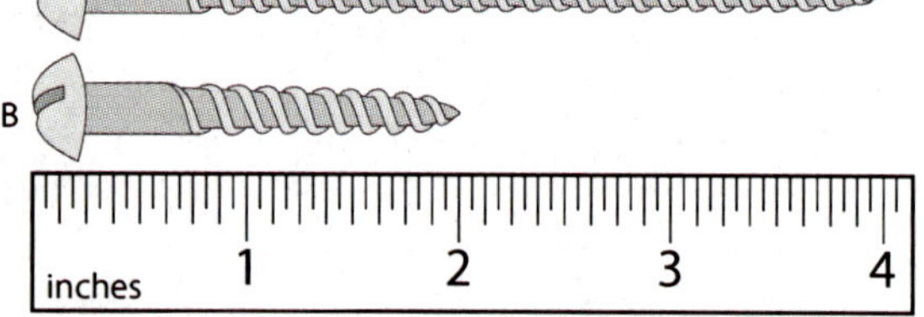

- How long is screw A?
- How long is screw B?
- How much longer is screw A than screw B?
- What is the sum of the two lengths?

6. Would a jet be 4 meters or 40 meters long?

7. 100 – 50 = ◯

8. What time is shown on the clock?

9. 70¢ – 18¢ = ?

10. Write the number using base-ten numerals.   98 tens

11. Mentally add 100.   216, 316, _____, _____, 616, _____

12. Which is greater, 2 quarters or 6 dimes?

13. What is the name of this shape?

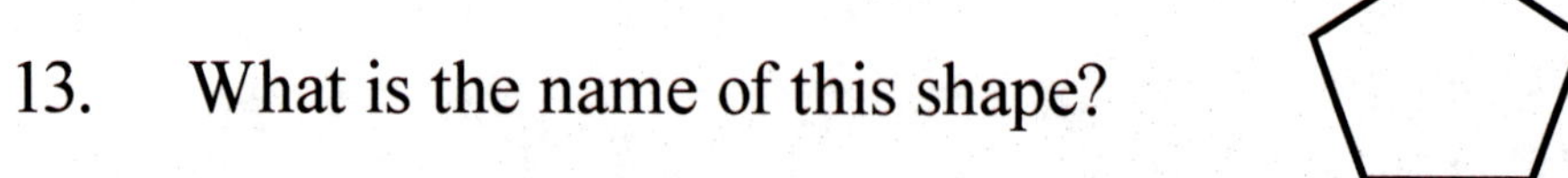

14. Fill in the sign to make this sentence true.   602 ◯ 612

15. 12 + 13 + 15 = ?

1. 2.MD.8	2. 2.OA.4	3. 2.NBT.7
4. 1.OA.7	5. 2.MD.4	6. 2.MD.3
7. 2.NBT.5	8. 2.MD.7	9. 2.MD.8
10. 2.NBT.3	11. 2.NBT.8	12. 2.MD.8
13. 2.G.1	14. 2.NBT.4	15. 2.NBT.6

Lesson #98

1. There were 24 cupcakes on the table at the beginning of the party. By the end of the party there were only 9 cupcakes left on the table. How many cupcakes were eaten during the party?

2. Count the objects in the array. Write an addition sentence to show the sum.

   _____ + _____ + _____ + _____ = _____

3. Is a basketball hoop about 9 feet tall or 9 inches tall?

4. How many cents do you have if you have two nickels, six pennies, and one quarter?

5. Would Marcy be able to throw the ball 31 feet or 312 feet?

6. Four-sided shapes with four angles are called _______.

   hexagons　　triangles　　quadrilaterals

7. Which tool would you use to find the length of computer screen in inches?　　scale　　thermometer　　measuring tape

8. Mr. McGarry's car is 16 feet long, Mrs. McGarry's car is 14 feet long, and Mike's car is 9 feet long. How long must the driveway be in order to fit all the cars parked from end to end? Write a number sentence and solve it.

9. 316 + 523 = ?

10. 60 − 24 = ?

11. 90 – 50 = ◯

12. 36 + 22 + 38 =

13. 5 + 9 = ?

14. Put these numbers in order from least to greatest.　　127　85　30　96　15

15. The same amount is shaded in which two rectangles? Draw them.

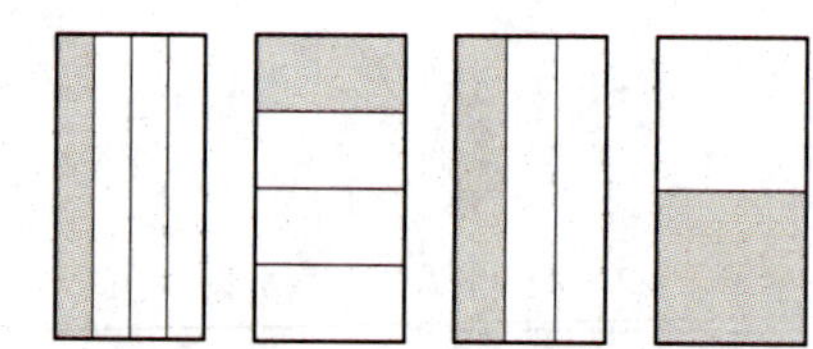

1. 2.OA.1	2. 2.OA.4	3. 2.MD.3
4. 2.MD.8	5. 2.MD.3	6. 2.G.1
7. 2.MD.1	8. 2.MD.5	9. 2.NBT.7
10. 2.NBT.5	11. 2.OA.1	12. 2.NBT.6
13. 2.OA.2	14. 2.NBT.4	15. 2.G.3

Lesson #99

1. Would you use a scale to find the width of a pillow in centimeters?

2. 28 + 16 + 35 = ?

3. The sum of two equal addends is an even number. Write the sums.

   9 + 9 = _____ 18 is an even number.
   7 + 7 = _____ 14 is an even number.
   3 + 3 = _____ 6 is an even number.

4. What number comes right after 605?

5. Is 39 closer to 30 or 40? Make a number line to help you.

6. Which two are equal?

   five dimes two quarters four nickels three quarters

7. A piece of string was 44 centimeters long. Roland cut off a length of 27 centimeters. How long was the piece that was left? Write a number sentence and solve it.

8. What number is 100 less than 884?

9. Would the new basketball court have hoops 40 feet or 10 feet high?

10. 654 − 32 = ?

11. What time is it?

12. 58 + 38 = ?

13. There are 98 students at Tree House Primary School. The kindergarten has 24 students, the first grade has 24 students, and the second grade has 24 students. How many students are in the third grade?

14. Choose the number that comes between 157 and 171.

    A) 132 B) 150 C) 164

15. What are the two most popular lunch foods?

    How many students like tacos and burgers best?

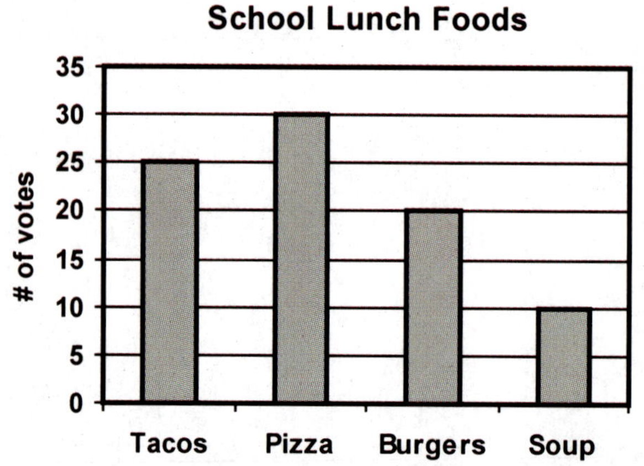

1. 2.MD.1	2. 2.NBT.6	3. 2.OA.3
4. 2.NBT.2	5. 3.NBT.1 (Prep)	6. 2.MD.8
7. 2.MD.5	8. 2.NBT.8	9. 2.MD.3
10. 2.NBT.7	11. 2.MD.7	12. 2.NBT.5
13. 2.OA.1	14. 2.NBT.2	15. 2.MD.10

Lesson #100

1. If you have a quarter, a dime, a nickel, and a penny, how many cents do you have?

2. Count the objects in the array. Write an addition sentence to show the sum.

   _____ + _____ + _____ + _____ + _____ = _____

3. Fill in the sign to make this sentence true. 964 ◯ 1,000

4. What number is 100 less than 987?

5. What number is ten less than 13? Write a number sentence.

   _____ – _____ = ◯

6. Trace over the dotted lines in the answer box. There are 5 rows. How many columns are there?

7. Write the number using base-ten numerals. 70 + 1 + 400

8. Would Matt's bicycle be 26 inches or 62 inches high?

9. 36 + 8 + 22 = ?

10. What time is it?

11. 354 – 44 = ?

12. Barb is wrapping packages with ribbon. One piece of ribbon is 18 inches long. Another piece is 27 inches long, and another piece is 32 inches long. How many inches of ribbon does Barb have all together? Write a number sentence and solve it.

13. Write the base-ten number for two hundred sixteen.

14. 15 – 6 = ?

15. Write your answers in inches.
    - How long is screw A?
    - How long is screw B?
    - How much shorter is screw B than screw A?
    - What is the sum of the two lengths?

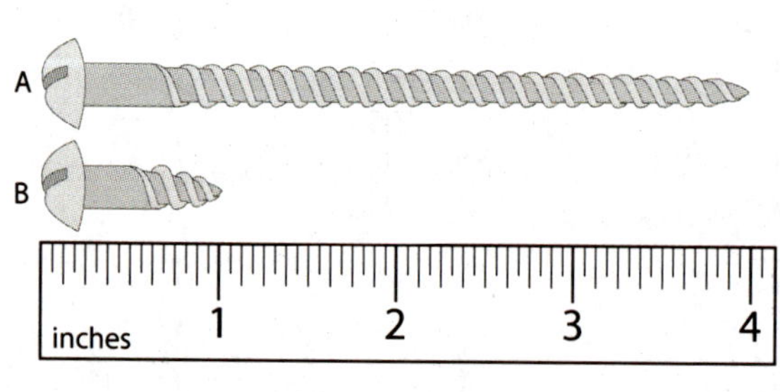

1. 2.MD.8	2. 2.OA.4	3. 2.NBT.4
4. 2.NBT.8	5. 2.OA.1	6. 2.G.2
7. 2.NBT.3	8. 2.MD.3	9. 2.NBT.5
10. 2.MD.7	11. 2.NBT.7	12. 2.MD.5
13. 2.NBT.3	14. 2.OA.2	15. 2.MD.4

Lesson #101

1. Count the objects in the array. Write an addition sentence to show the sum.

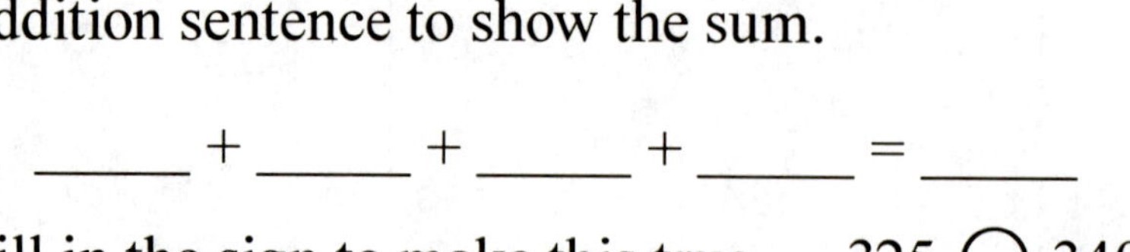

_____ + _____ + _____ + _____ = _____

2. Fill in the sign to make this true. 325 ◯ 340

3. Would you use a tape measure to find the length of a dance floor in feet?

4. Write the name of the shape in the box. How many faces does it have?

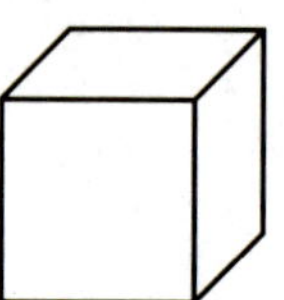

5. Match the amounts that are equal.

_____ 36¢	A) a dime, a nickel, and ten pennies
_____ 29¢	B) a quarter, a nickel, and six pennies
_____ 25¢	C) two dimes and nine pennies

6. Would the front door be 3 feet or 30 feet wide?

7. Write the number using base-ten numerals. 9 tens

8. The answer to an addition problem is the __________.

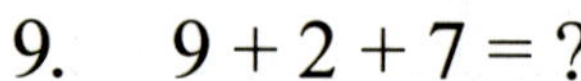

9. 9 + 2 + 7 = ?

10. This circle is divided into two equal shares, called __________.

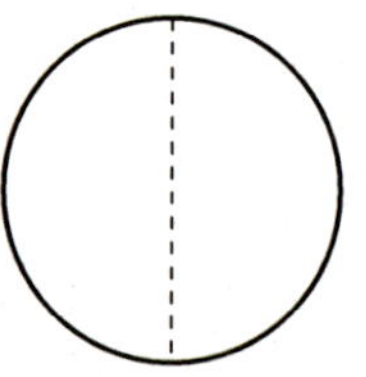

11. 456 − 36 = ?

12. Fill in the missing numbers. 230, ____, 250, ____, ____

13. Charlie's number is five less than 14. What is Charlie's number?

14. 615 + 332 = ?

15. Write your answers in inches.

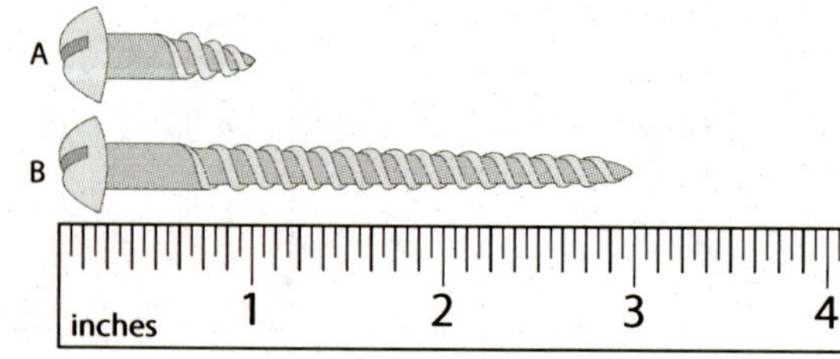

- How long is screw A?
- How long is screw B?
- How much longer is screw B than screw A?
- What is the sum of the two lengths?

1. 2.OA.4	2. 2.NBT.4	3. 2.MD.1
4. 2.G.1	5. 2.MD.8	6. 2.MD.3
7. 2.NBT.3	8. 1.OA.7	9. 2.OA.2
10. 2.G.3	11. 2.NBT.7	12. 2.NBT.2
13. 2.OA.1	14. 2.NBT.7	15. 2.MD.4

Lesson #102

1. Find the egg on page 152 of your Hands-On pages. Measure its height to the nearest centimeter.

2. Count the objects in the array. Write an addition sentence to show the sum.

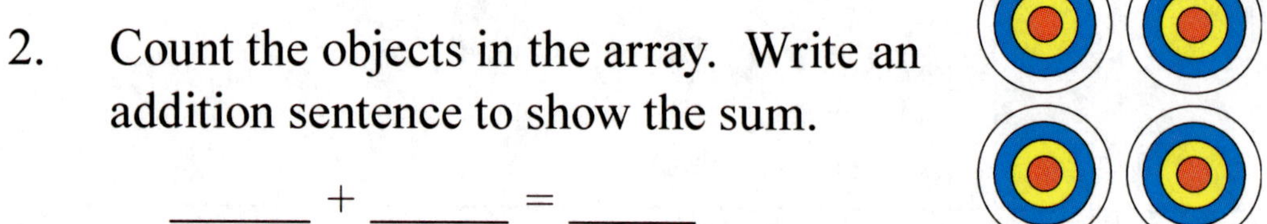

   _____ + _____ = _____

3. Mentally add 100. 473, 573, _____, _____, _____, 973

4. 5 + 6 is the same as ____ + 8. Both are equal to 11.

5. 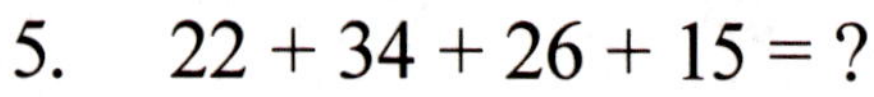 22 + 34 + 26 + 15 = ?

6.  25 + _____ = 77

7. Write this as a base-ten numeral.
   4 ones, 6 hundreds, and 8 tens

8. Derek rode his bike 16 miles on Monday, 20 miles on Wednesday, and 14 miles on Thursday. How many miles did Derek ride all together? Write a number sentence and solve it.

9. Would the bedroom ceiling be 3 meters or 30 meters high?

10. Trace over the dotted lines in the answer box. There are 3 columns. How many rows are there?

11. Chan has 68¢. His mother gives him 3 dimes and then he buys a pencil for 18¢. How much money does he have now?

12. Is 29 closer to 20 or to 30?

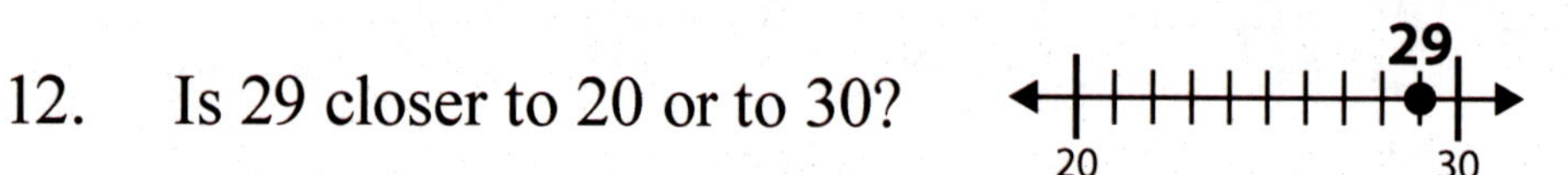

13. 553 + 214 = ?

14. What time is it?

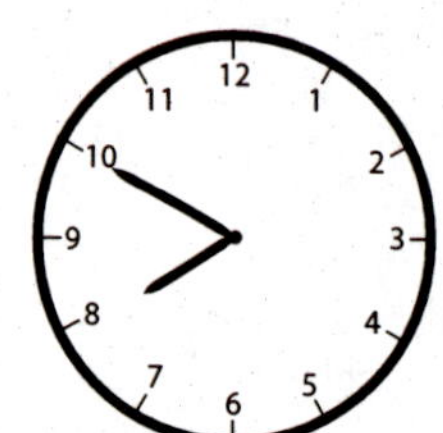

15. 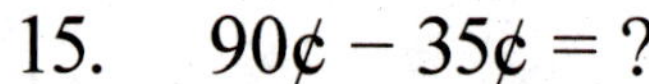 90¢ − 35¢ = ?

1. 2.MD.3	2. 2.OA.4	3. 2.NBT.8
4. 2.OA.2	5. 2.NBT.6	6. 2.OA.1
7. 2.NBT.3	8. 2.MD.5	9. 2.MD.3
10. 2.G.2	11. 2.MD.8	12. 3.NBT.1 (Prep)
13. 2.NBT.7	14. 2.MD.7	15. 2.MD.8

Lesson #103

1. The sum of two equal addends is an even number. Write the sums.

   2 + 2 = _____　　4 + 4 = _____　　6 + 6 = _____

   4 is an even number.　　8 is an even number.　　12 is an even number.

2. 53 + 9 = ?

3. Write the number using base-ten numerals. 28 tens

4. Trace over the dotted lines in the answer box. There are 2 rows. How many columns are there ?

5. There are 15 muffins on a plate. Eight of them are banana muffins. How many are <u>not</u> banana muffins?

6. Would we meet my aunt for lunch at 11:30 a.m. or 11:30 p.m.?

7. 657 − 242 = ?

8. Write the time shown on the clock.

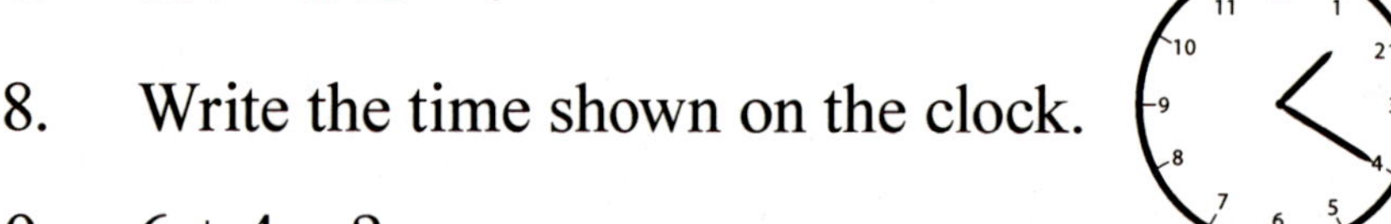

9. 6 + 4 = ?

10. Fill in the sign to make this sentence true. 66 ◯ 121

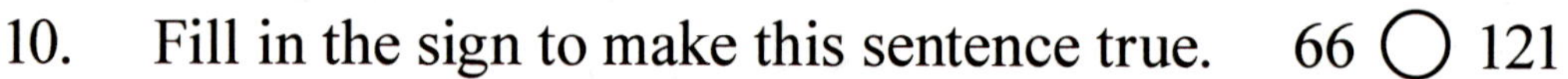

11. Which is greater, 2 dollars or 9 quarters?

12. Which shapes are divided into three equal thirds? Draw them.

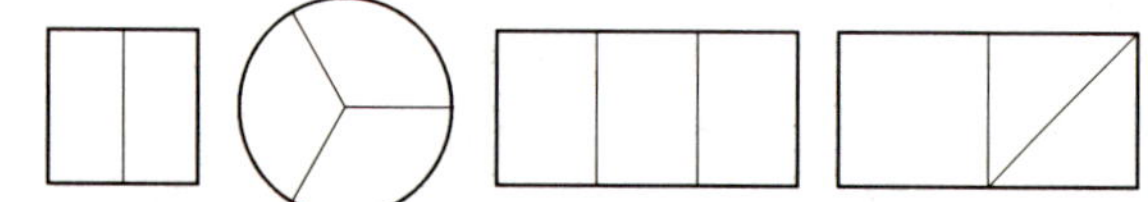

13. A bicycle path is 45 miles long. Jin rode 28 miles before lunch and 13 miles after lunch. How much farther will Jin have to ride to get to the end of the bicycle path? Write a number sentence and solve it.

14. Write the number 209 using words.

15. Write your answers in inches.

   - How long is screw A?
   - How long is screw B?
   - How much shorter is screw B than screw A?
   - What is the sum of the two lengths?

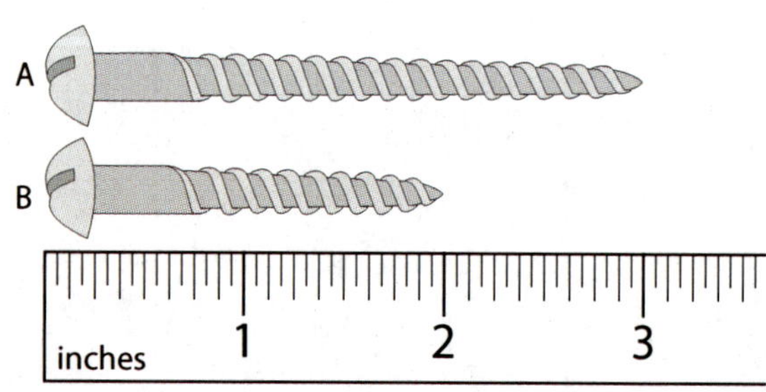

1. 2.OA.3	2. 2.NBT.5	3. 2.NBT.3
4. 2.G.2	5. 2.OA.1	6. 2.MD.7
7. 2.NBT.7	8. 2.MD.7	9. 2.OA.2
10. 2.NBT.4	11. 2.MD.8	12. 2.G.3
13. 2.MD.5	14. 2.NBT.3	15. 2.MD.4

Lesson #104

1. Trace over the dotted lines in the answer box. There is 1 column. How many rows are there?

2. Would you use a compass to find the width of a parking lot in meters?

3. Which two are equal?

   five nickels　　two dimes　　one dollar　　a quarter

4. Write the name of this shape.

   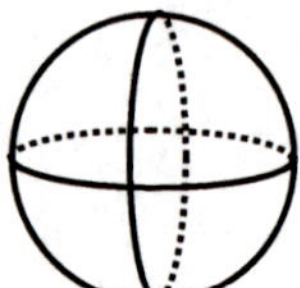

   sphere　　cube　　cone

5. Would the floor lamp be 5 feet or 15 feet high?

6. Mentally add 100.　573, 673, _____, _____, _____

7. Second and third graders use the playground at recess. Mrs. Rice counted 15 second graders. When the bell rang, 23 students lined up to go inside. How many of them were third graders?

8. Billie's desk is 29 inches wide. Randy's desk is 32 inches wide. Can the desks fit in a space that is 65 inches wide? Write a number sentence and solve it.

9. $640 - 320 = ?$

10. $15 + 26 + 38 = ?$

11. Write 93 using words.

12 – 15. Finn asked his classmates whether they would rather have a dog or a cat as a pet. Use the information in Finn's data chart to make a picture graph. (See the *Help Pages*.)

Type of Pet	Votes
Dog	6
Cat	8

- Give the graph a title.
- Write a label on each side of the graph.
- Fill in the picture graph key. Show ♥ = 1 vote.
- Draw the correct number of ♥ for each type of pet.

1. 2.G.2

2. 2.MD.1

3. 2.MD.8

4. 1.G.2

5. 2.MD.3

6. 2.NBT.8

7. 2.OA.1

8. 2.MD.5

9. 2.NBT.7

10. 2.NBT.6

11. 2.NBT.3

12 – 15. 2.MD.10

____

Dog	
Cat	

____

Key:

Lesson #105

1. 518 + 271 = ?

2. What shape has five sides and five angles? Draw one in the box.

3. Grace is six years older than Suzy. Suzy is five years old. How old is Grace?

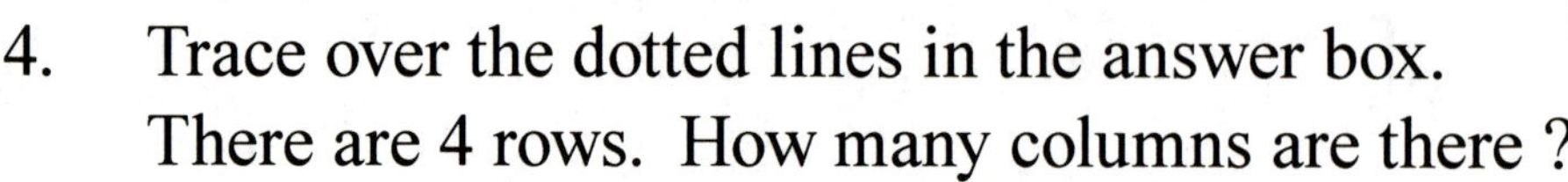

4. Trace over the dotted lines in the answer box. There are 4 rows. How many columns are there ?

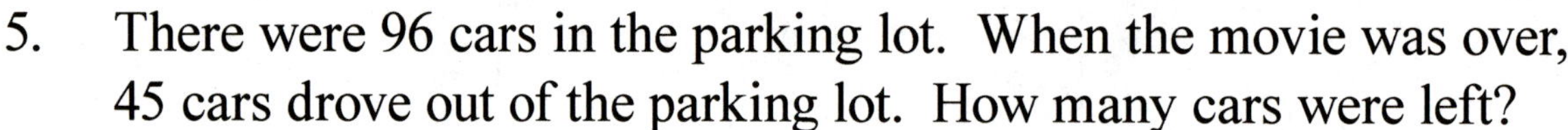

5. There were 96 cars in the parking lot. When the movie was over, 45 cars drove out of the parking lot. How many cars were left?

6. If you have a quarter and two dimes, how many cents do you have?

7. Would the driveway be 20 centimeters or 20 meters long?

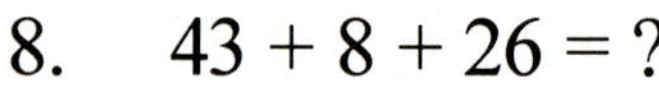

8. 43 + 8 + 26 = ?

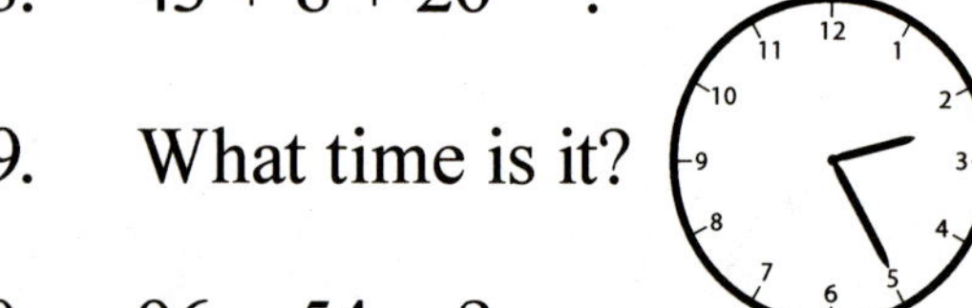

9. What time is it?

10. 96 − 54 = ?

11. Is an envelope about 9 inches long or 9 feet long?

12. Fill in the sign to make this sentence true. 304 ◯ 329

13. Count by fives. 65, 70, _____, _____, 85, _____, 95

14. What base-ten number is this? 500 + 80 + 6

15. Write your answers in inches.
    - How long is screw A?
    - How long is screw B?
    - How much longer is screw A than screw B?

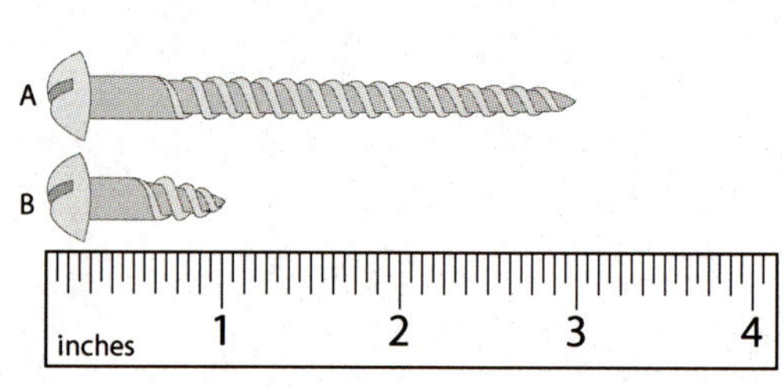

1. 2.NBT.7	2. 2.G.1	3. 2.OA.1
4. 2.G.2	5. 2.OA.1	6. 2.MD.8
7. 2.MD.3	8. 2.NBT.5	9. 2.MD.7
10. 2.NBT.5	11. 2.MD.3	12. 2.NBT.4
13. 2.NBT.2	14. 2.NBT.3	15. 2.MD.4

Lesson #106

1. 44 − 16 = ?
2. The sum of two equal addends is an even number. Write the sums.

   1 + 1 = _____ 2 is an even number.

   5 + 5 = _____ 10 is an even number.

   7 + 7 = _____ 14 is an even number.
3. 9 + 7 is the same as 8 + _____. Both are equal to 16.
4. The answer to a subtraction problem is the __________.
5. Frank had 39 baseball cards. He sold 11 cards, and he gave 12 cards to his brother. How many baseball cards does Frank have left? Write a number sentence and solve it.
6. 713 + 65 = ?
7. Is 16 closer to 10 or 20?

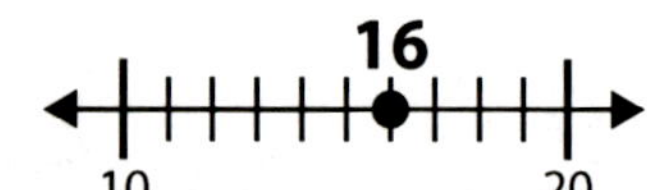

8. The rectangle in the answer box has 2 same-size rows and 4 same-size columns. Put one X in each square. How many Xs are there? This number tells you the number of square units.
9. Write your answers in inches.
   - How long is branch A?
   - How long is branch B?
   - How much longer is branch A than branch B?

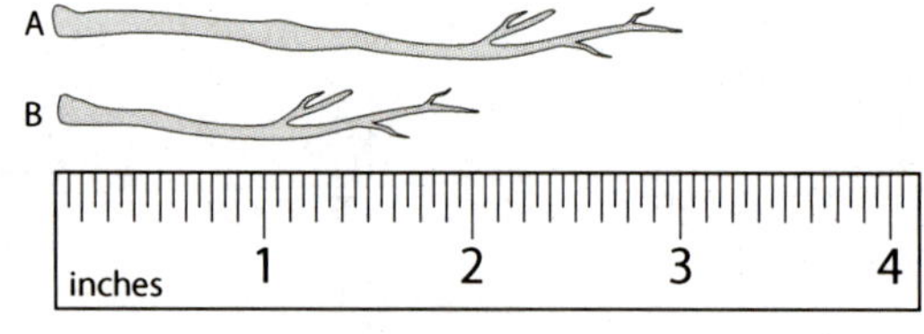

10. If you have 7 dimes and 2 nickels, how much money do you have?
11. 24 + 13 + 8 = ?
12. Count the objects in the array. Write the addition sentence to show the sum.

_____ + _____ + _____ + _____ = _____

13. Write the number using base-ten numerals. 34 tens
14. Write the missing numbers in the sequence. 15, 20, _____, 30, _____
15. Is this figure a cube?

1. 2.NBT.5	2. 2.OA.3	3. 2.OA.2
4. 1.OA.7	5. 2.OA.1	6. 2.NBT.7
7. 3.NBT.1 (Prep)	8. 2.G.2	9. 2.MD.4
10. 2.MD.8	11. 2.NBT.5	12. 2.OA.4
13. 2.NBT.3	14. 2.NBT.2	15. 1.G.2

Lesson #107

1. Find the iguana on page 152 of your Hands-On pages. Measure its length to the nearest centimeter.

2. 60¢ − 31¢ = ?

3. What time is it?

4. 7 + 9 = ?

5. If you have a dollar bill, four quarters, and two hundred pennies, do you have more or less than five dollars?

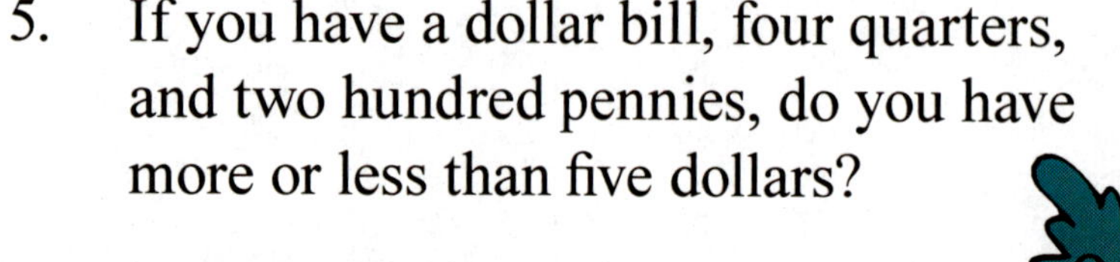

6. Write the base-ten number for six hundred twenty-nine.

7. Would you use a thermometer or a meter stick to find the length of a bed in centimeters?

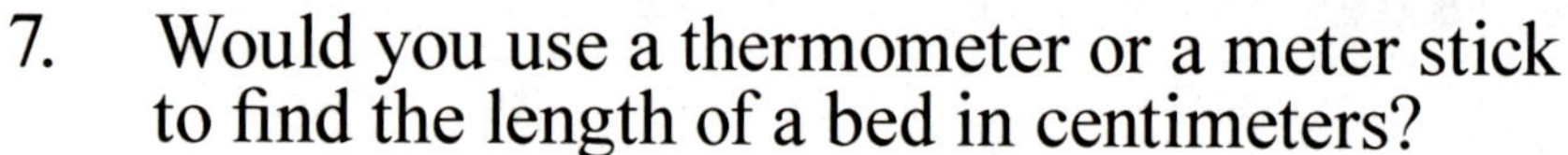

8. Mr. Carter's yard is 55 feet wide. Ms. Lang's yard is 62 feet wide. How much wider is Ms. Lang's yard? Write a number sentence and solve it.

9. What number does the symbol stand for? 85 + ♠ = 100

10. Finish the pattern. 200, 300, ____, 500, 600, ____, 800, ____, 1,000

11. The difference is the answer to a(n) ________ problem.

12. Write the number that has 3 hundreds, 5 tens, and 2 ones.

13. Fill in the sign to make this sentence true. 480 ◯ 590

14. 121 + 65 = ?

15. How many bags of leaves were collected on Tuesday and Thursday?

On which day were the most bags collected?

Leaf Collection

Day	Bags Collected
Monday	
Tuesday	
Wednesday	
Thursday	
Friday	

Each stands for 2 bags

1. 2.MD.3	2. 2.MD.8	3. 2.MD.7
4. 2.OA.2	5. 2.MD.8	6. 2.NBT.3
7. 2.MD.1	8. 2.MD.5	9. 2.OA.1
10. 2.NBT.2	11. 1.OA.7	12. 2.NBT.3
13. 2.NBT.4	14. 2.NBT.7	15. 2.MD.10

Lesson #108

1. What is the best tool for measuring how many inches long your toothbrush is?

balance calculator ruler

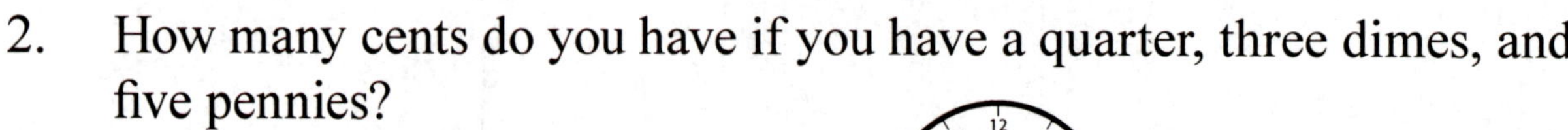

2. How many cents do you have if you have a quarter, three dimes, and five pennies?

3. What time is shown on the clock?

4. 58 + 29 = ?

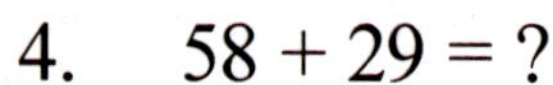

5. 19 – _____ = 7

6. In which two rectangles are equal amounts shaded? Draw them.

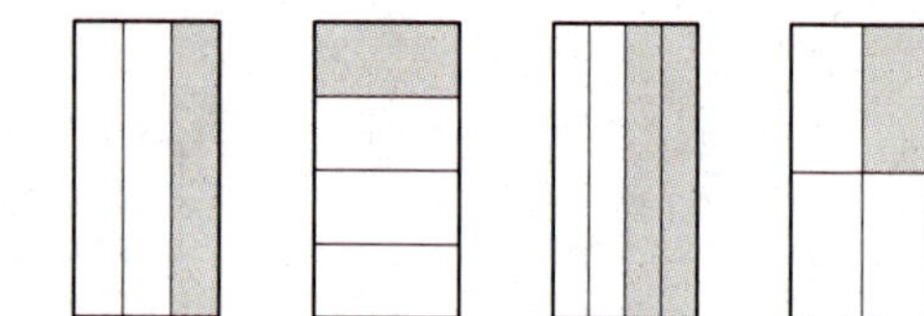

7. Mrs. Lind is 65 inches tall, and her son, Hakeem, is 57 inches tall. How much taller is Mrs. Lind than Hakeem? Write a number sentence and solve it.

8. Is 11 closer to 10 or 20?

9. 736 – 24 = ?

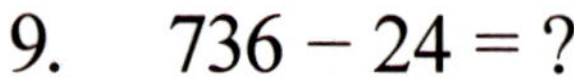

10. What is the name of this shape?

11. Would a fire truck be 4 feet or 40 feet long?

12. Write the number using base-ten numerals. 14 tens and 4 ones

13. The rectangle in the answer box has 3 same-size rows and 5 same-size columns. How many square units are there ?

14. Count the objects in the array. Write an addition sentence to show the sum.

_____ + _____ + _____ + _____ + _____ = _____

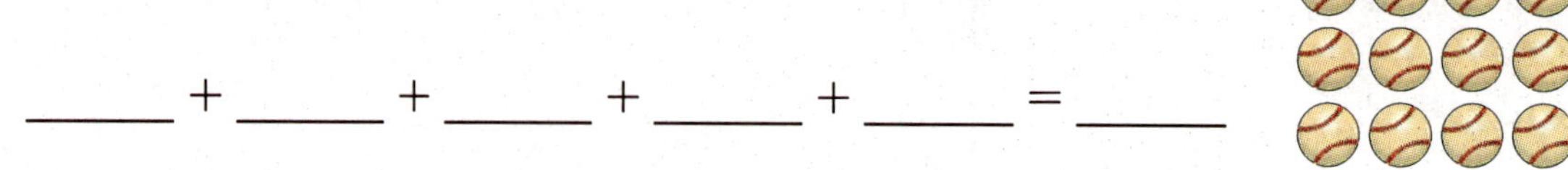

15. What number is ten more than 60? Write a number sentence.

1. 2.MD.1	2. 2.MD.8	3. 2.MD.7
4. 2.NBT.5	5. 2.OA.1	6. 2.G.3
7. 2.MD.3	8. 3.NBT.1 (Prep)	9. 2.NBT.7
10. 2.G.1	11. 2.MD.3	12. 2.NBT.3
13. 2.G.2	14. 2.OA.4	15. 2.NBT.8

Lesson #109

1. 346 + 153 = ?
2. Draw 2 quadrilaterals.
3. Would a can of soda be closer to 5 inches or 12 inches high?
4. **The measure of how long something takes to happen is called *elapsed time.***

   The movie began at 4:00. It ended at 6:00. How long did the movie last?

5. What number is 17 less than 18?
6. Corey wants to make a belt that is 25 inches long. She has a piece of leather that is 56 inches long. If Corey cuts the belt from the piece of leather, how many inches will be left over? Write a number sentence and solve it.
7. Draw a circle that is divided into two equal halves.
8. What number is 100 less than 903?
9. 475 − 133 = ?
10. Which heart is divided into 2 equal parts? Draw it.

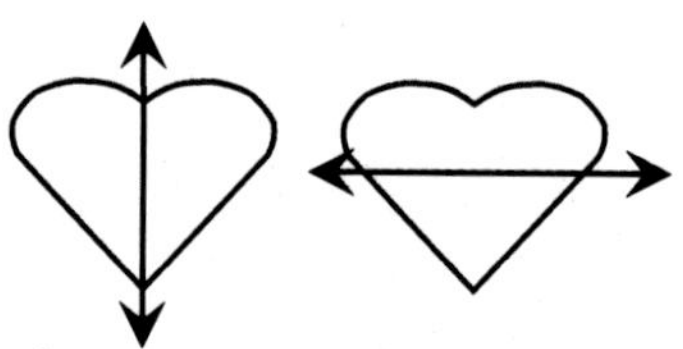

11. What base-ten number is this? 100 + 70 + 4
12. Fill in the sign to make this sentence true. 893 ◯ 887
13. Which is greater, 2 quarters or 6 dimes?
14. The pet store had 27 goldfish for sale. The owner sold nine goldfish on Thursday and ten goldfish on Friday. How many goldfish were left?
15. Write your answers in inches.
    - How long is branch A?
    - How long is branch B?
    - How much shorter is branch B than branch A?

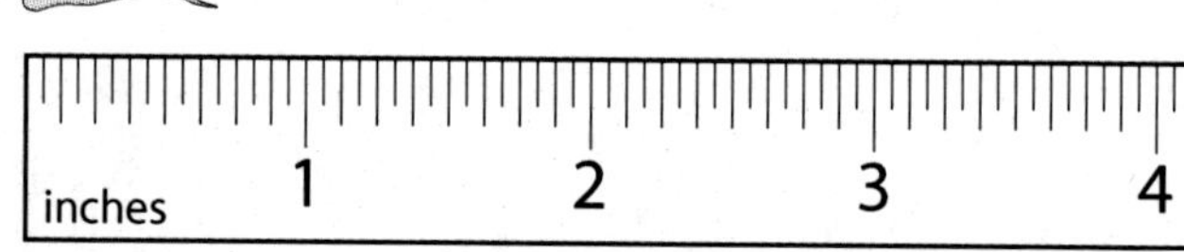

1. 2.NBT.7	2. 2.G.1	3. 2.MD.3
4. 2.MD.7	5. 2.OA.1	6. 2.MD.5
7. 2.G.3	8. 2.NBT.8	9. 2.NBT.7
10. 2.G.3	11. 2.NBT.3	12. 2.NBT.4
13. 2.MD.8	14. 2.OA.1	15. 2.MD.4

Lesson #110

1. The rectangle in the answer box has 4 same-size rows and 3 same-size columns. How many square units are there ?

2. What number is 100 more than 350?

3. What is the name of this figure? How many faces does it have?

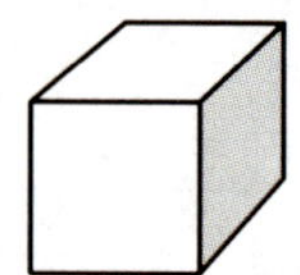

4. Fill in the missing numbers. 45, _____, 65, _____, 85

5. If you have three dollar bills, a quarter, and four dimes, how much is that?

   \$3 and 75¢   \$3 and 65¢   \$3 and 95¢   \$3 and 25¢

6. 10 + 10 + 10 + 10 is the same as 20 + 20. Both are equal to ________.

7. 97 – 68 = ?

8. 45 + 26 + 8 = ?

9. What time is it?

10. 36¢ + 19¢ = ?

11. Write the number using base-ten numerals. 29 tens and 2 ones

12. Would the bed blanket be 60 inches or 16 inches wide?

13. Write the base-ten number for six hundred forty-seven.

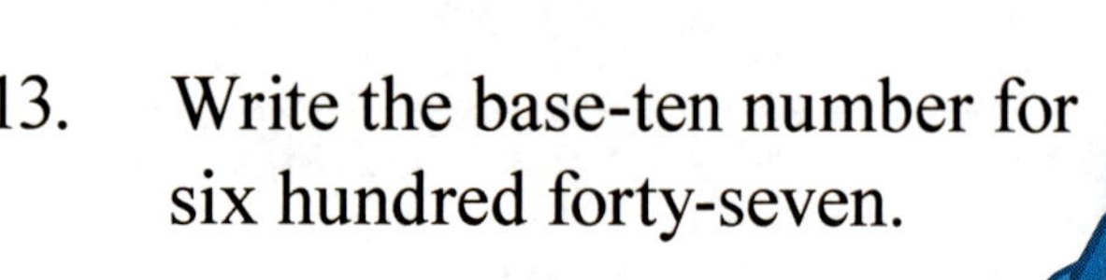

14. What number does the symbol stand for? ◆ + 14 = 18

15. Find the fork on page 152 of your Hands-On pages. Measure its length to the nearest centimeter.

1. 2.G.2	2. 2.NBT.8	3. 2.G.1
4. 2.NBT.2	5. 2.MD.8	6. 2.NBT.5
7. 2.NBT.5	8. 2.NBT.5	9. 2.MD.7
10. 2.MD.8	11. 2.NBT.3	12. 2.MD.3
13. 2.NBT.3	14. 2.OA.1	15. 2.MD.3

Lesson #111

1. The rectangle in the answer box has 1 row and 2 same-size columns. How many square units are there?

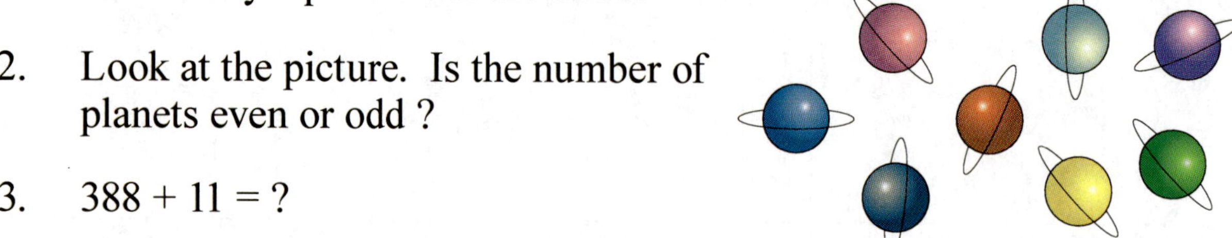

2. Look at the picture. Is the number of planets even or odd ?

3. 388 + 11 = ?

4. Beth's number is four less than 16. What is Beth's number?

5. The concert began at 8:00. It ended at 10:00. How long did the concert last?

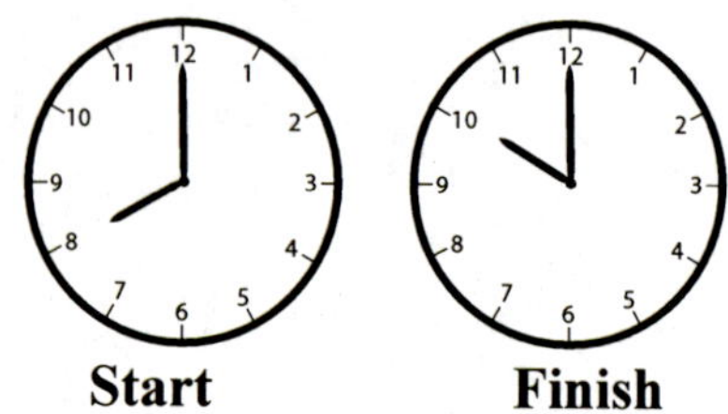

6. How much money is 10 quarters?

7. Fill in the sign to make this sentence true. 464 ◯ 644

8. Which shape has six sides and six angles?

9. Would the leaf be 4 inches or 40 inches across?

10. 6 + 9 = ?

11. The sum is the answer to a(n) ____________ problem.

12 – 15. Cam visited an aquarium and counted three different types of fish. Use the information in Cam's data chart to make a picture graph. (See the *Help Pages*.)

- Give the graph a title.
- Write labels on the left side and bottom of the graph.
- Fill in the picture graph key. Show = 1 fish.
- Draw the correct number of symbols next to the label for each type of fish.

Fish Type	# of Fish
Angelfish	5
Blowfish	2
Clownfish	4

1. 2.G.2	2. 2.OA.3	3. 2.NBT.7
4. 2.OA.1	5. 2.MD.7	6. 2.MD.8
7. 2.NBT.4	8. 2.G.1	9. 2.MD.3
10. 2.OA.2	12 – 15. 2.MD.10	
11. 1.OA.7		

Angelfish	
Blowfish	
Clownfish	

Key:

Lesson #112

1. Jackie's dad made 36 hotdogs for the class picnic. There were 24 children and 6 adults. If everyone had one hotdog, how many were left over?

2. 518 + 261 = ?

3. What time is it?

4. Write the symbol that tells you to subtract.

5. Which number follows 99?

6. Count by tens. 50, 60, ______, ______, 90, ______

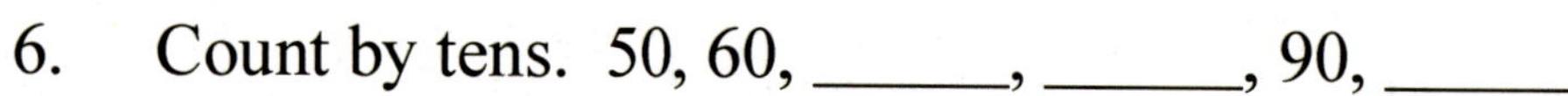

7. Count the objects in the array. Write an addition sentence to show the sum.

______ + ______ + ______ + ______ = ______

8. If you have ten dimes and ten pennies, do you have more or less than a dollar?

9. 750 − 320 = ?

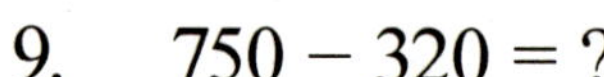

10. This square is divided into two equal shares, called ________.

11. Fill in the sign to make this sentence true. 434 ◯ 443

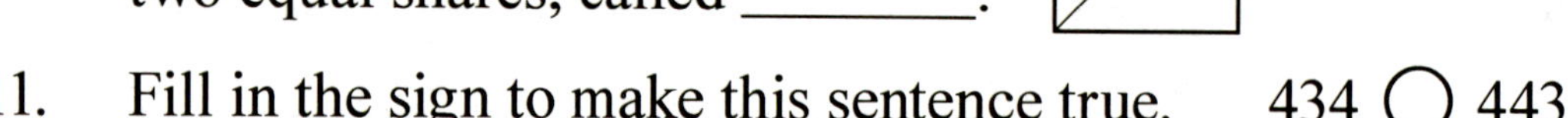

12. A stack of three boxes is 54 inches high. One box is 16 inches tall and another is 17 inches tall. How tall is the third box?

13. Write the number using base-ten numerals. 1 + 70 + 100

14. Ellen bought a pen for \$2.50 and a tablet for \$1.35. How much money did Ellen spend on these supplies?

15. Write your answers in inches.
   - How long is nail A?
   - How long is nail B?
   - How much longer is nail A than nail B?

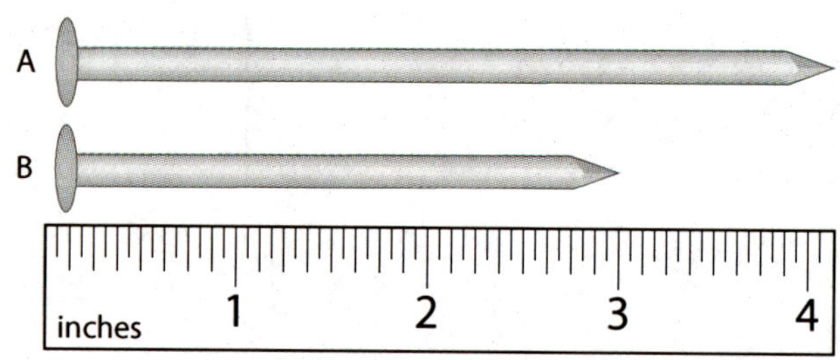

1. 2.OA.1	2. 2.NBT.7	3. 2.MD.7
4. 1.OA.7	5. 2.NBT.2	6. 2.NBT.2
7. 2.OA.4	8. 2.MD.8	9. 2.NBT.7
10. 2.G.3	11. 2.NBT.4	12. 2.MD.5
13. 2.NBT.3	14. 2.MD.8	15. 2.MD.4

Lesson #113

1. 37 + 35 = ?

2. 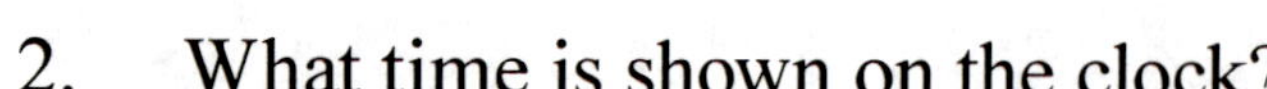 What time is shown on the clock?

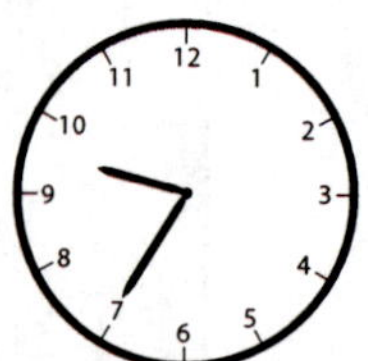

3. Write 176 using words.

4. Write the number using base-ten numerals.　48 tens and 6 ones

5. The rectangle in the answer box has 4 same-size rows and 5 same-size columns. How many square units are there?

6. The sum of two equal addends is an even number. Write the sums.

   6 + 6 = _____　　8 + 8 = _____　　2 + 2 = _____
   12 is an even number.　　16 is an even number.　　4 is an even number.

7. Find Pencil D on page 153 of your Hands-On pages. Measure its length to the nearest centimeter.

8. What number does the symbol stand for?　65 − ★ = 60

9. Nicki measured her grandmother's vegetable garden. It was 3 meters long. What tool did Nicki use to measure?

10. The play began at 8:00 p.m. and ended at 11:00 p.m. How long was the play?

Start

Finish

11. 724 − 303 = ?

12. The sum is the answer to a(n) __________ problem.

13. Write this using base-ten numerals.　Three hundred seventy-five

14. How many cents do you have if you have a quarter, two nickels and five pennies?

15. Ron is making a birdhouse. He needs three more pieces of wood. One piece must be 13 inches long, another must be 15 inches long, and the last one must be 17 inches long. How many inches of wood does Ron need to build the birdhouse? Write a number sentence and solve it.

1. 2.NBT.5	2. 2.MD.7	3. 2.NBT.3
4. 2.NBT.3	5. 2.G.2	6. 2.OA.3
7. 2.MD.3	8. 2.OA.1	9. 2.MD.1
10. 2.MD.7	11. 2.NBT.7	12. 1.OA.7
13. 2.NBT.3	14. 2.MD.8	15. 2.MD.5

Lesson #114

1. Casey's dresser is 36 inches wide and her desk is 42 inches wide. How many inches of space will Casey need if she wants to put the dresser and the desk side by side? Write a number sentence and solve it.

2. 556 + 322 = ?

3. Would a horse's tail be 48 inches or 84 inches long?

4. Write the symbol that tells you to subtract.

5. Joey counted 12 tulips in the front yard and more in the back yard. All together, there were 26 tulips. How many tulips were in the back yard?

6. Draw 2 quadrilaterals.

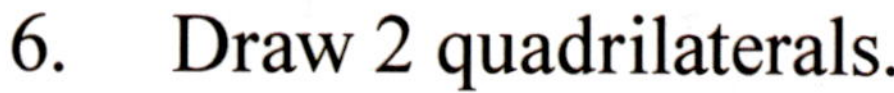

7. How much time has passed?

Start

Finish

8. 84 − 29 = ?

9. This circle is divided into two equal parts. What do we call the two parts?

10. Write the name of each shape.

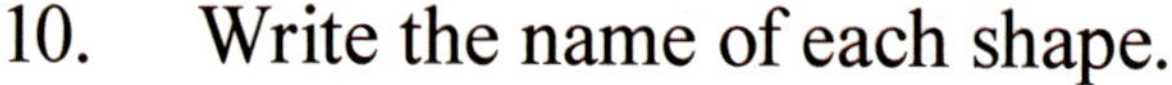

A) 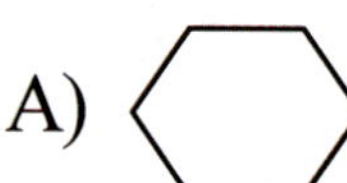 B)  C) 

11. Count by 100s. 500, 600, ______, ______, ______, 1,000

12. Count the objects in the array. Write an addition sentence to show the sum.

______ + ______ + ______ + ______ = ______

13. What number is six less than 56? Write a number sentence.

14. Is 71 closer to 70 or 80?

15. Write the number using base-ten numerals. 18 tens and 1 one

1. 2.MD.5	2. 2.NBT.7	3. 2.MD.3
4. 1.OA.7	5. 2.OA.1	6. 2.G.1
7. 2.MD.7	8. 2.NBT.5	9. 2.G.3
10. 2.G.1	11. 2.NBT.2	12. 2.OA.4
13. 2.OA.1	14. 3.NBT.1 (Prep)	15. 2.NBT.3

Lesson #115

1. A school bus can hold 55 students. There are 23 students in Mr. North's class and 36 students in Mrs. Willaman's class. Will both classes be able to fit on one school bus?

2. What shape has three sides and three angles?

3. Fill in a sign to make this sentence true. 316 ◯ 163

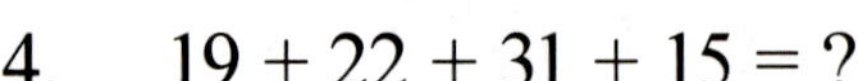

4. 19 + 22 + 31 + 15 = ?

5. Which number comes between 135 and 230? 415 121 205

6. Use the grid paper in the answer box. Draw a rectangle that has three equal rows and two equal columns. How many square units are in the rectangle?

7. Mark wants to know how wide the garage door is. What tool should Mark use to measure it?

   meter stick tape measure yardstick any of these

8. How much money do you have if you have 8 nickels?

9. Which shape is divided into two equal halves? Draw it.

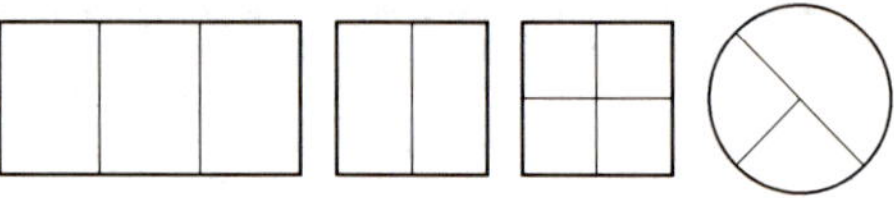

10. Write the number using base-ten numerals. 31 tens and 4 ones

11. 259 − 44 = ?

12. Write the time shown on the clock.

13. What number is 100 less than 365?

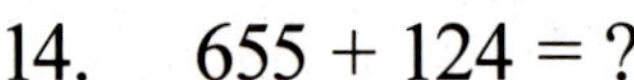

14. 655 + 124 = ?

15. Whose swim lesson is the longest?

    What time is the 6 – 9 year-old lesson?

Swim Lessons	
Age (yrs.)	Time
3 - 5	9:00 – 9:30
6 - 9	9:30 – 10:00
10	10:00 – 11:00

1. 2.OA.1	2. 2.G.1	3. 2.NBT.4
4. 2.NBT.6	5. 2.NBT.2	6. 2.G.2
7. 2.MD.1	8. 2.MD.8	9. 2.G.3
10. 2.NBT.3	11. 2.NBT.7	12. 2.MD.7
13. 2.NBT.8	14. 2.NBT.7	15. 2.MD.10

Lesson #116

1. Write this as a base-ten numeral. Nine hundred ninety-nine

2. 700 has _____ hundreds, _____ tens, and _____ ones.

3. What number is two more than 11? Write a number sentence.

_____ + _____ = ◯

4. Fill in the sign to make this sentence true. 356 ◯ 295

5. What is the name of the shape?

6. Count the objects in the array. Write an addition sentence to show the sum.

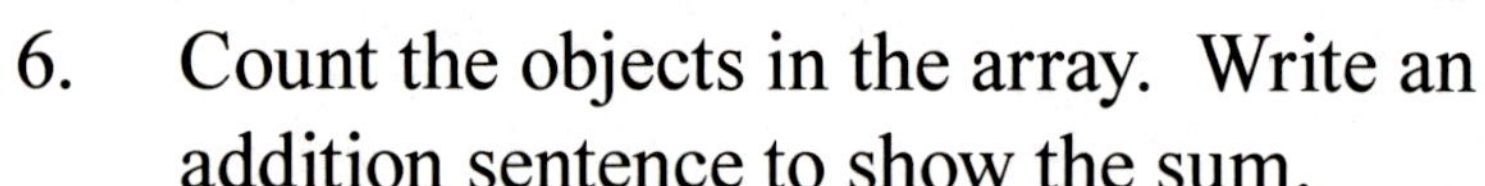

_____ + _____ + _____ + _____ + _____ = _____

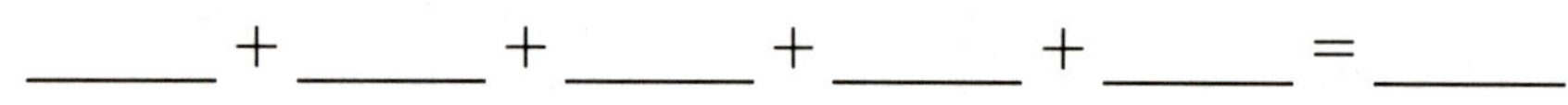

7. Quadrilaterals have how many sides and angles?

8. Mrs. Thomas's house has three floors. There are 15 rooms on the first floor, 14 rooms on the second floor, and 15 rooms on the third floor. How many rooms are in Mrs. Thomas's house?

9. If you have a nickel, a dime, and seven pennies, how many cents do you have?

10. Write the time shown on the clock.

11. Find Pencil F on page 153 of your Hands-On pages. Measure its length to the nearest centimeter.

12. 759 − 239 = ?

13. Draw a rectangle that is divided into two equal halves.

14. 14 + 12 + 22 = ?

15. Would a sub sandwich be 8 inches or 80 inches long?

1. 2.NBT.3	2. 2.NBT.1	3. 2.OA.1
4. 2.NBT.4	5. 2.G.1	6. 2.OA.4
7. 2.G.1	8. 2.OA.1	9. 2.MD.8
10. 2.MD.7	11. 2.MD.3	12. 2.NBT.7
13. 2.G.3	14. 2.NBT.6	15. 2.MD.3

Lesson #117

1. There were one hundred twenty-five people at the zoo on Friday. There were two hundred sixty-six people at the zoo on Saturday. How many people were at the zoo on Friday and Saturday?

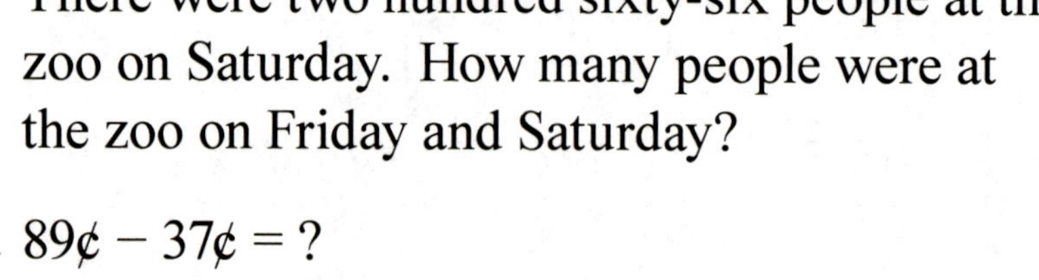

2. 89¢ − 37¢ = ?

3. 62 + _____ = 87

4. Is a couch about 6 inches long or 6 feet long?

5. Write the number using base-ten numerals. 11 tens

6. When Brian was born, his parents planted a seedling that was 15 inches tall. Now it has grown into a tree that is 48 inches tall. How many inches has the tree grown since it was planted? Write a number sentence and solve it.

7. 564 + 235 = ?

8. The concert began at 2:00 and ended at 4:00. How long did the concert last?

9. Write two equal addends. _____ + _____ = 2

10. Fill in the missing numbers. 230, 240, _____, 260, _____

11. Fill in a sign to make this sentence true. 527 ◯ 257

12 – 15. Mei asked 14 friends to choose a favorite snow cone flavor. Use the information in Mei's data chart to make a picture graph. (See the *Help Pages*.)

- Give the graph a title.
- Write labels on the left side and bottom of the graph.
- Fill in the picture graph key. Show ▽ = 1 vote.
- Draw the correct number of symbols next to the label for each flavor.

Snow Cone Flavors	# of Votes
Cherry	3
Lemon	5
Blueberry	2
Orange	4

1. 2.OA.1

2. 2.MD.8

3. 2.OA.1

4. 2.MD.3

5. 2.NBT.3

6. 2.MD.3

7. 2.NBT.7

8. 2.MD.7

9. 2.OA.3

10. 2.NBT.2

11. 2.NBT.4

12 – 15. 2.MD.10

____

Cherry	
Lemon	
Blueberry	
Orange	

____

Key:

Lesson #118

1. 353 − 132 = ?

2. Write the time shown on the clock.

3. Match the amounts that are equal.

_____	40¢	A) a quarter, a dime, and a nickel
_____	65¢	B) a quarter and four pennies
_____	29¢	C) six dimes and five pennies

4. Kwan's number is 14 less than 24. What is Kwan's number?

5. Fill in the sign to make this sentence true. 314 ◯ 167

6. What base-ten number is this? 800 + 40 + 9

7. 43 + 29 = ?

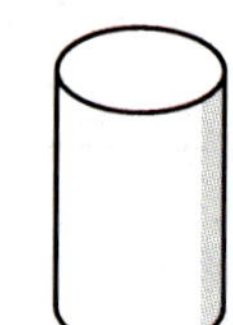

8. What is the name of this shape?

9. There were 345 people at the water park on Thursday. On Friday, 675 people visited the water park. How many more people were at the water park on Friday than on Thursday?

10. Find Pencil J on page 153 of your Hands-On pages. Measure its length to the nearest centimeter.

11. Which number comes just before 1,000?

12. Write 597 using words.

13. The answer to a subtraction problem is the ________.

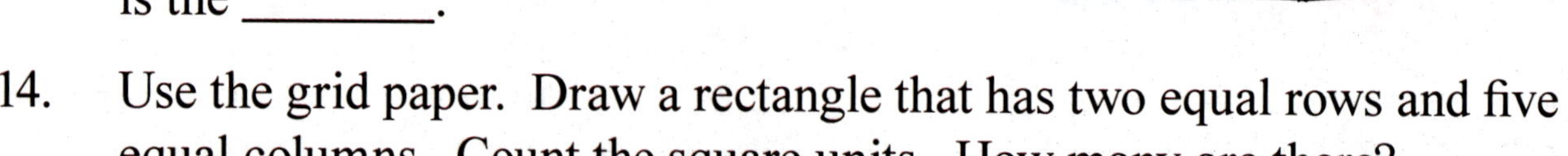

14. Use the grid paper. Draw a rectangle that has two equal rows and five equal columns. Count the square units. How many are there?

15. Write your answers in centimeters.
   - How long is line A?
   - How long is line B?
   - How much shorter is line A than line B?

1. 2.NBT.7	2. 2.MD.7	3. 2.MD.8
4. 2.OA.1	5. 2.NBT.4	6. 2.NBT.3
7. 2.NBT.5	8. 1.G.2	9. 2.OA.1
10. 2.MD.3	11. 2.NBT.2	12. 2.NBT.3
13. 1.OA.7	14. 2.G.2	15. 2.MD.4

Lesson #119

1. Marsha planted a row of seeds in her garden. The whole row was 90 centimeters long. If Marsha used the first 45 centimeters for pumpkin seeds, how many centimeters did she use for squash seeds? Write a number sentence and solve it.

2. Write the name of the shape.

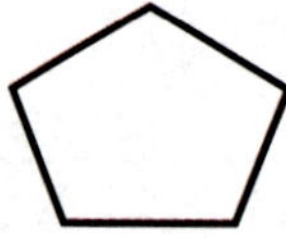

3. 25 + 14 + 26 + 10 = ?

4. Is 68 closer to 60 or 70?

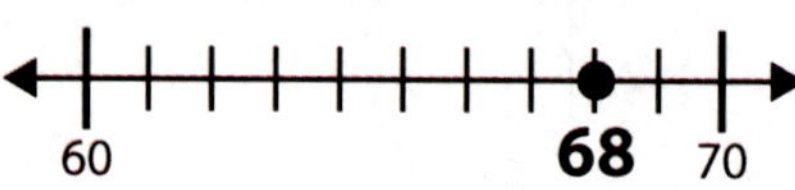

5. 533 + 455 = ?

6. How much time has passed?

Start

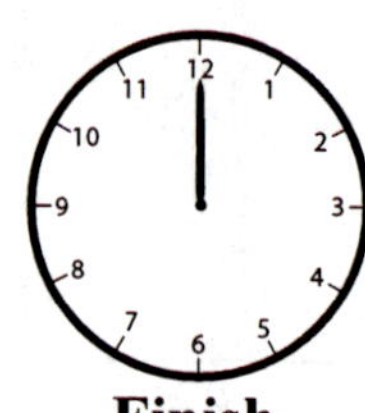

Finish

7. 637 − 305 = ?

8. Draw a rectangle that has four equal rows and three equal columns. How many square units are in the rectangle?

9. Count the objects in the array. Write an addition sentence to show the sum.

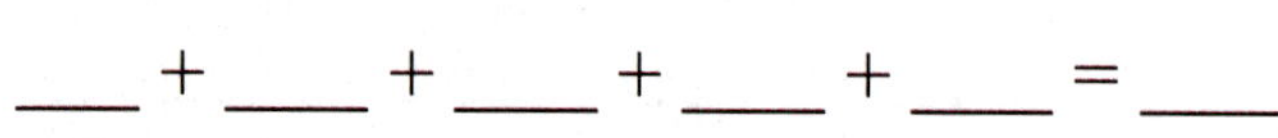

___ + ___ + ___ + ___ + ___ = ___

10. The sum is the answer to a(n) __________ problem.

11. Write two equal addends. _____ + _____ = 12

12. Which two are equal?

    three quarters　　one dollar　　twenty nickels　　five dimes

13. Fill in the sign to make this sentence true. 114 ◯ 98

14. What number is 100 less than 201?

15. Which class is the longest? How long is it?

    What time does math class start?

Class Schedule	
8:30 – 9:00	Spelling
9:00 – 10:00	Reading
10:00 – 10:30	Math
10:30 – 11:00	English

1. 2.MD.5	2. 2.G.1	3. 2.NBT.6
4. 3.NBT.1 (Prep)	5. 2.NBT.7	6. 2.MD.7
7. 2.NBT.7	8. 2.G.2	9. 2.OA.4
10. 1.OA.7	11. 2.OA.3	12. 2.MD.8
13. 2.NBT.4	14. 2.NBT.8	15. 2.MD.10

Lesson #120

1. 325 + 464 = ?

2. Write the time shown on the clock.

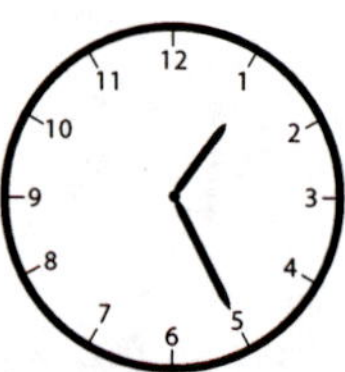

3. 19 + 33 + 41 = ?

4. 7 + 8 = 9 + _____. Both are equal to 15.

5. Draw a rectangle that has two equal rows and two equal columns. How many square units are in the rectangle?

6. Write the number using base-ten numerals. 91 tens

7. Fill in the sign to make this sentence true. 983 ◯ 1,000

8. Write two equal addends. _____ + _____ = 8

9. Find Pencil K on page 153 of your Hands-On pages. Measure its length to the nearest centimeter.

10. If you have three dimes, fifty pennies, and one quarter, do you have more or less than one dollar?

11. The tank in Mr. Lester's car holds 18 gallons of gasoline. When Mr. Lester filled the tank, he only needed to add 7 gallons of gas. How many gallons of gas were already in the tank?

12. What number does the symbol stand for? ☽ + 27 = 27

13. Is a telephone about 8 inches long or 8 feet long?

14. 798 – 254 = ?

15. A hiking path is 22 miles long. Mindy hiked 10 miles on the first day and 7 miles on the second day. How many more miles will Mindy have to hike to finish the trail?

1. 2.NBT.7	2. 2.MD.7	3. 2.NBT.6
4. 2.OA.2	5. 2.G.2	6. 2.NBT.3
7. 2.NBT.4	8. 2.OA.3	9. 2.MD.3
10. 2.MD.8	11. 2.OA.1	12. 2.OA.1
13. 2.MD.3	14. 2.NBT.7	15. 2.MD.5

Lesson #121

1. Gloria's shoe rack is 18 inches wide. Her closet wall is 26 inches wide. How many inches of space will be left over if Gloria puts the shoe rack against the wall in her closet?

2. Is 88 closer to 80 or 90?

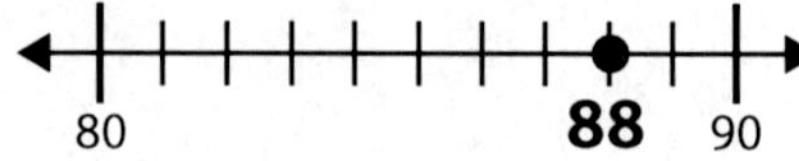

3. 36 + 25 + 12 = ?

4. If you have three dollar bills, eight quarters, and two pennies, do you have more or less than five dollars?

5. 728 – 314 = ?

6. What time is it?

7. 333 + 466 = ?

8. Fill in the sign to make this sentence true. 324 ◯ 254

9. Write the number using base-ten numerals. 66 tens and 7 ones

10. Put the numbers in order from least to greatest.

    365 254 987 125

11. This rectangle is divided into three equal parts, called ________.

12. Which of these is the best tool for measuring the length of a fork?

    meter stick teaspoon ruler air pump

13. Write your answers in centimeters.
    - How long is line R?
    - How long is line S?
    - How much shorter is line S than line R?

R ————

S ——

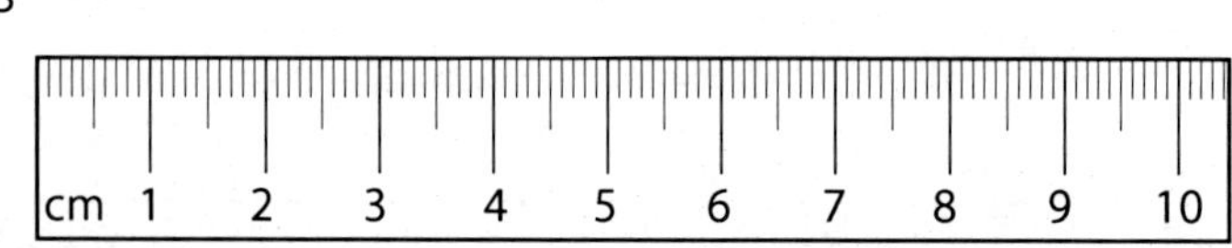

14. Write the number using base-ten numerals. 400 + 7 + 30

15. How many children chose apples?

    How many more children chose grapes than peaches?

Favorite Fruits	
Fruit	**Votes**
Apples	𝍸 𝍸
Bananas	////
Grapes	𝍸 //
Peaches	///

1. 2.MD.5	2. 3.NBT.1 (Prep)	3. 2.NBT.6
4. 2.MD.8	5. 2.NBT.7	6. 2.MD.7
7. 2.NBT.7	8. 2.NBT.4	9. 2.NBT.3
10. 2.NBT.4	11. 2.G.3	12. 2.MD.1
13. 2.MD.4	14. 2.NBT.3	15. 2.MD.10

Lesson #122

1. A stack of blocks is 27 inches high. One block is 7 inches tall and another is 9 inches tall. How tall is the third block?

2. Count the objects in the array. Write an addition sentence to show the sum.

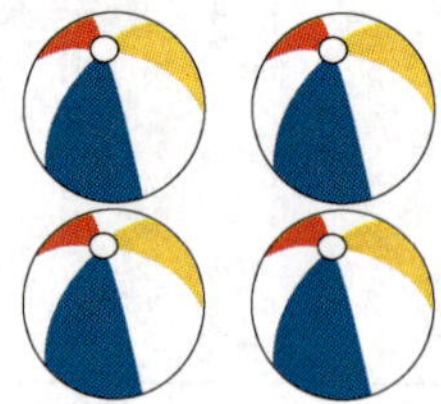

_____ + _____ = _____

3. Would Deena's baby picture in her dad's wallet be 12 inches or 2 inches high?

4. Write the name of the shape.

5. Write two equal addends. _____ + _____ = 18

6. Mentally add 100. 216, 316, _____, _____, 616, _____, 816

7. 69¢ + 23¢ = ?

8. What is the time shown on the clock?

9. 757 − 136 = ?

10. The same amount is shaded in which two rectangles? Draw them.

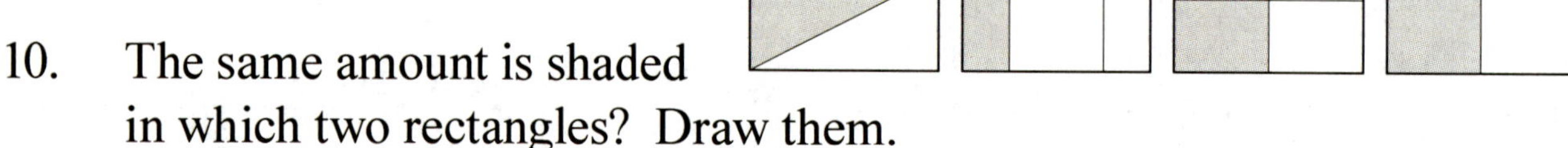

11. Fill in the sign to make this sentence true. 510 ◯ 317

12. Count by fives. 75, ____, 85, ____, ____

13. Draw a rectangle that has five equal rows and four equal columns. How many square units are in the rectangle?

14. Lee read 28 pages on Monday. He read 16 pages on Tuesday and 23 more pages on Wednesday. How many pages did Lee read during the three days?

15. Write this as a base-ten numeral.
Seven hundred twenty

1. 2.MD.5	2. 2.OA.4	3. 2.MD.3
4. 1.G.2	5. 2.OA.3	6. 2.NBT.8
7. 2.MD.8	8. 2.MD.7	9. 2.NBT.7
10. 2.G.3	11. 2.NBT.4	12. 2.NBT.2
13. 2.G.2	14. 2.OA.1	15. 2.NBT.3

Lesson #123

1. How much money is 5 quarters?

2. This circle is divided into three equal shares, called ________.

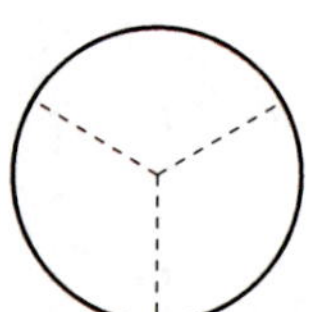

3. Write the number using base-ten numerals. 60 + 5 + 900

4. 3 + 8 = ?

5. How much time has passed?

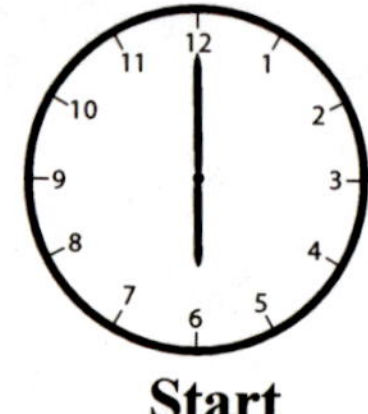

Start

Finish

6. 406 + 572 = ?

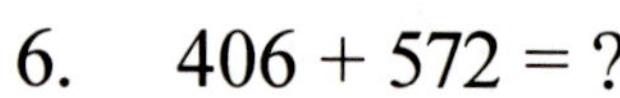

7. What number is three more than 58? Write a number sentence.

8. The sum is the answer to a(n) __________ problem.

9. 734 − 224 = ?

10. Write the name of this shape. How many faces does it have?

11. Fill in the sign to make this sentence true. 777 ◯ 946

12. A bridge is 67 feet long. Mr. Ally painted the first 20 feet on Monday and the next 30 feet on Tuesday. How many more feet of bridge will Mr. Ally have to paint to finish the bridge?

13. 27 + 18 + 11 + 33 = ?

14. Draw a rectangle that has three equal rows and one column. How many square units are in the rectangle?

15. Write your answers in centimeters.
    - How long is line O?
    - How long is line P?
    - How much longer is line O than line P?

1. 2.MD.8	2. 2.G.3	3. 2.NBT.3
4. 2.OA.2	5. 2.MD.7	6. 2.NBT.7
7. 2.OA.1	8. 1.OA.7	9. 2.NBT.7
10. 2.G.1	11. 2.NBT.4	12. 2.MD.5
13. 2.NBT.6	14. 2.G.2	15. 2.MD.4

Lesson #124

1. Fill in the sign to make this sentence true. 743 ◯ 786

2. Leon used 3 feet of string on one kite, 2 feet for another kite, and 3 feet for a third kite. He had 12 feet of string left. How many feet of string did he begin with?

3. 408 + 561 = ?

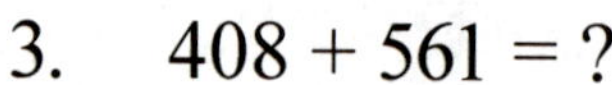

4. 25 + 25 + 42 = ?

5. 918 – 203 = ?

6. 75 + _____ = 90

7. Write 427 using words.

8. Is 21 closer to 20 or 30?

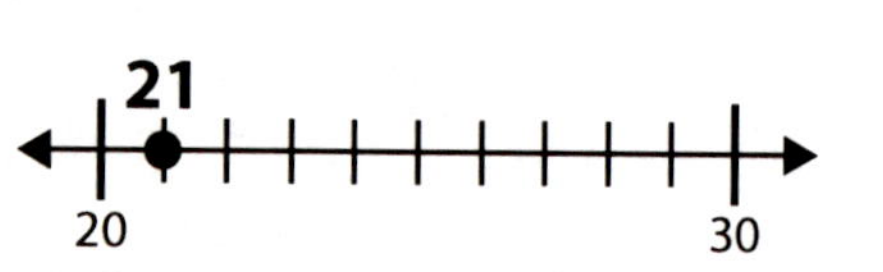

9. What number is 100 less than 459?

10. Would Suzi be 7 inches or 70 inches shorter than her best friend?

11. Arrange these numbers from greatest to least. 813 650 142 436

12. If you have six dollar bills, a quarter, and three dimes, how much is that?

    $6 and 35¢ $6 and 30¢ $7 and 30¢ $6 and 55¢

13. Eleven students measured the lengths of their shoes. The line plot shows the results. How many shoes measured under 7 inches? How long were most students' shoes?

Lengths of Shoes in Inches

5 6 7 8 9

14. Is your desk 3 inches tall or 3 feet tall?

15. Write the base-ten number for five hundred sixty-two.

1. 2.NBT.4	2. 2.MD.5	3. 2.NBT.7
4. 2.NBT.6	5. 2.NBT.7	6. 2.OA.1
7. 2.NBT.3	8. 3.NBT.1 (Prep)	9. 2.NBT.8
10. 2.MD.3	11. 2.NBT.4	12. 2.MD.8
13. 2.MD.9	14. 2.MD.3	15. 2.NBT.3

Lesson #125

1. Twelve students measured the height of their bean sprout plants on day five. The line plot shows the results. How many plants measured 3 cm or higher? How tall were most students' plants?

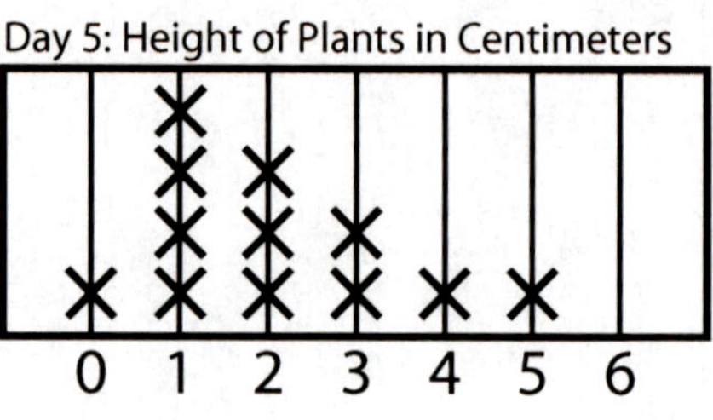

2. Is 43 closer to 40 or 50?

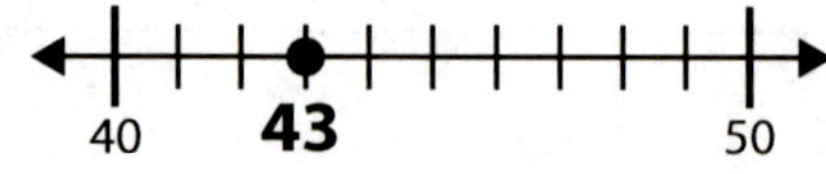

3. 345 + 543 = ?

4. The answer to an addition problem is the ________.

5. How much money do you have if you have 6 quarters?

6. Count the objects in the array. Write an addition sentence to show the sum.

_____ + _____ + _____ = _____

7. 859 – 246 = ?

8. Draw a rectangle that has one row and three equal columns. How many square units are in the rectangle?

9. What number does the symbol stand for? 97 – ♠ = 93

10. Write this number. 8 tens, 4 hundreds, 6 ones

11. Fill in the sign to make this sentence true. 375 ◯ 257

12. How much time has passed?

13. 2 + 4 + 9 = ?

14. Count by tens. 240, 250, _____, _____, 280

15. Write your answers in centimeters.
   - How long is line B?
   - How long is line C?
   - How much shorter is line B than line C?

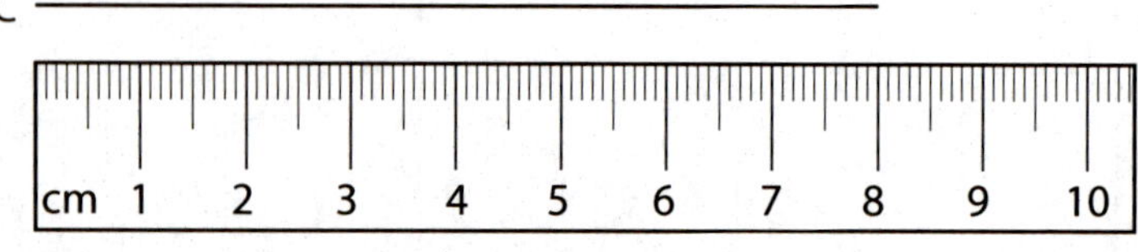

1. 2.MD.9	2. 3.NBT.1 (Prep)	3. 2.NBT.7
4. 1.OA.7	5. 2.MD.8	6. 2.OA.4
7. 2.NBT.7	8. 2.G.2	9. 2.OA.1
10. 2.NBT.3	11. 2.NBT.4	12. 2.MD.7
13. 2.OA.2	14. 2.NBT.2	15. 2.MD.4

Lesson #126

1. $9 + 7 = ?$

2. Write the time shown on the clock.

3. Write your answers in centimeters.
   - How long is A?
   - How long is B?
   - How much shorter is A than B?

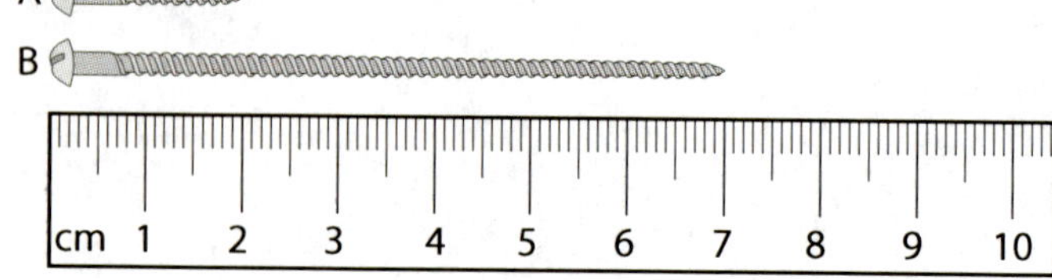

4. A fence is 39 feet long. Marsha painted the first 15 feet on Monday and the next 10 feet on Tuesday. How many more feet will Marsha have to paint to finish the fence?

5. Count the objects in the array. Write an addition sentence to show the sum.

   _____ + _____ = _____

6. Write the number using base-ten numerals. 6 tens

7. What number is 100 less than 809?

8. Write two equal addends. _____ + _____ = 4

9. $637 - 114 = ?$

10. What is the name of the shape that has four sides and four angles?

    pentagon quadrilateral hexagon

11. Fill in the sign to make this sentence true. 475 ◯ 324

12. Draw a rectangle that has four equal rows and three equal columns. How many square units are in the rectangle?

13. Write the base-ten number for three hundred twenty-nine.

14. $537 + 262 = ?$

15. Jason planted 25 seeds in one carton and 18 seeds in another carton. How many seeds did Jason plant in all?

1. 2.OA.2	2. 2.MD.7	3. 2.MD.4
4. 2.MD.5	5. 2.OA.4	6. 2.NBT.3
7. 2.NBT.8	8. 2.OA.3	9. 2.NBT.7
10. 2.G.1	11. 2.NBT.4	12. 2.G.2
13. 2.NBT.3	14. 2.NBT.7	15. 2.OA.1

Lesson #127

1. Write this number using base-ten numerals. Four hundred twelve

2. If you have seven dimes and two quarters, do you have more or less than a dollar?

3. 314 + 485 = ?

4. Put the numbers in order from least to greatest. 27, 10, 39, 19, 41

5. Write two equal addends. _____ + _____ = 14

6. Write the number using base-ten numerals. 79 tens and 4 ones

7. A café is 42 feet wide and its parking lot is 58 feet wide. How many feet wide are the café and parking lot together?

8. Draw a rectangle that has three equal rows and four equal columns. How many square units are in the rectangle?

9. The ______ is the answer to a subtraction problem.

10. Is this figure a cube?

11. 852 − 322 = ?

12 – 15. Frasier counted three kinds of trees at the park. Use the information in Frasier's data chart to make a bar graph. (See the *Help Pages*.)

- Give the graph a title.
- Fill in the numbers for the left side of the graph. Zero is given. Go up by 1s.
- Write labels on the left side and bottom of the graph.
- Draw the bars to the correct height. Label each bar.

Type of Tree	# of Trees
Oak	6
Maple	5
Elm	3

1. 2.NBT.3	2. 2.MD.8	3. 2.NBT.7
4. 2.NBT.4	5. 2.OA.3	6. 2.NBT.3
7. 2.MD.5	8. 2.G.2	9. 1.OA.7
10. 2.G.1	12 – 15. 2.MD.10	
11. 2.NBT.7		

0

Lesson #128

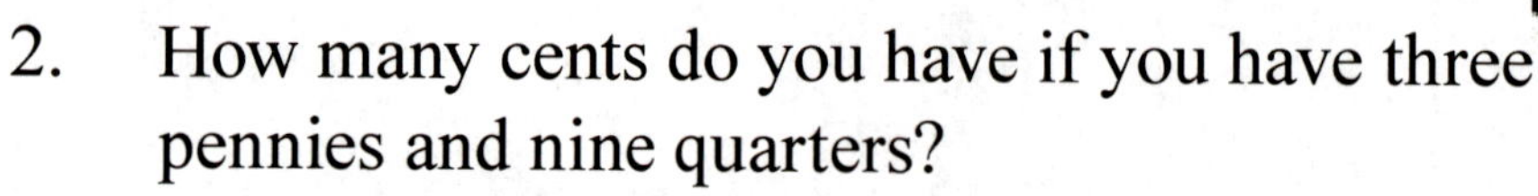

1. The sum is the answer to a(n) _____ problem.

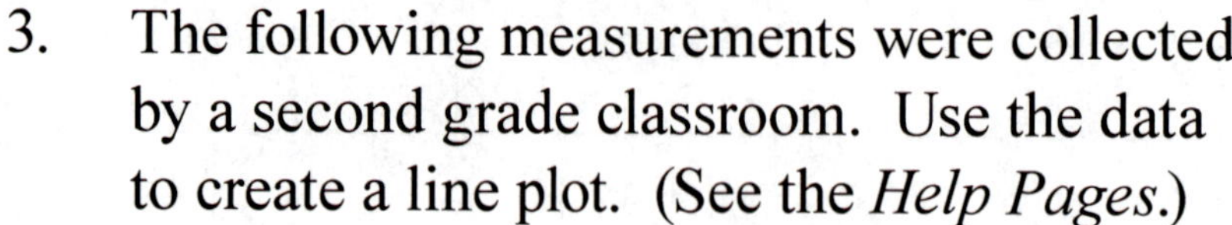

2. How many cents do you have if you have three pennies and nine quarters?

3. The following measurements were collected by a second grade classroom. Use the data to create a line plot. (See the *Help Pages*.)

Student Arm Length

Student	Length (cm)
Matt	54
Connie	58
Devon	56
Julius	52
Ming	54
Whitney	56
Sarah	54
Angel	55

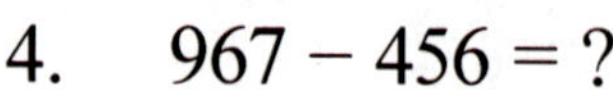

4. 967 − 456 = ?

5. Write 534 using words.

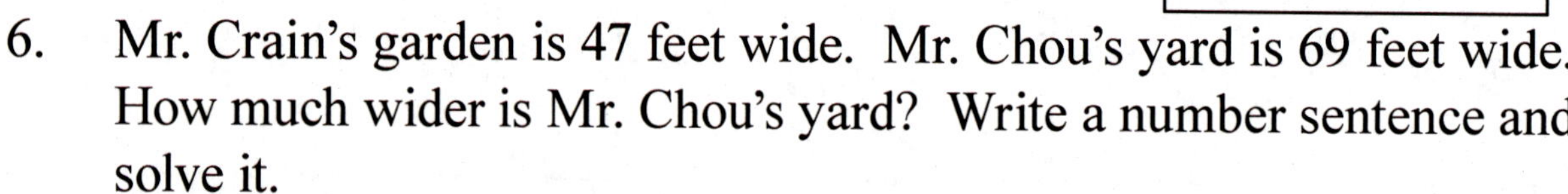

6. Mr. Crain's garden is 47 feet wide. Mr. Chou's yard is 69 feet wide. How much wider is Mr. Chou's yard? Write a number sentence and solve it.

7. Fill in the missing numbers. 365, ____, 385, ____

8. Draw a circle that is divided into three equal thirds.

9. 68¢ + 27¢ = ?

10. How much time has passed?

Start

Finish

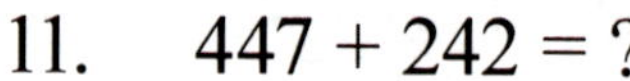

11. 447 + 242 = ?

12. Write the number using base-ten numerals. 2 + 700 + 20

13. Which is longer, 9 inches or 1 foot?

14. Count the objects in the array. Write an addition sentence to show the sum.

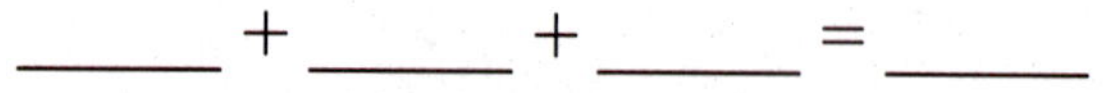

_____ + _____ + _____ = _____

15. Write your answers in centimeters.
   - How long is line C?
   - How long is line D?
   - How much shorter is line C than line D?

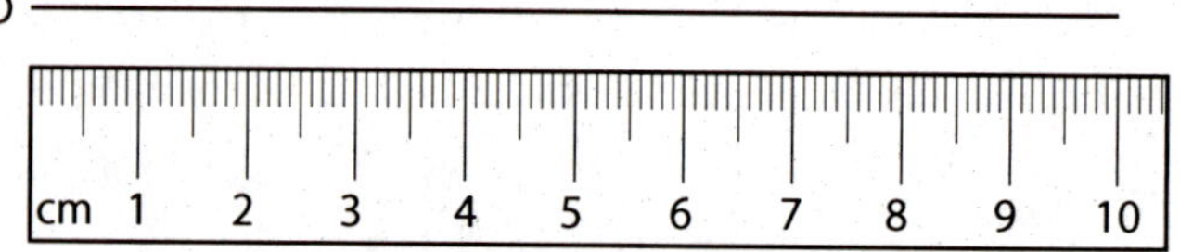

1. 1.OA.7	2. 2.MD.8	3. 2.MD.9 Arm Length 52 53 54 55 56 57 58
4. 2.NBT.7	5. 2.NBT.3	6. 2.MD.5
7. 2.NBT.2	8. 2.G.3	9. 2.MD.8
10. 2.MD.7	11. 2.NBT.7	12. 2.NBT.3
13. 2.MD.3	14. 2.OA.4	15. 2.MD.4

Lesson #129

1. Write the number using base-ten numerals. 45 tens

2. Fill in the sign to make this sentence true. 312 ◯ 231

3. 566 − 243 = ?

4. There were 165 marbles in the jar. Jason gave 88 of those marbles to his friend Ryan. How many marbles are left in the jar?

5. 721 + 238 = ?

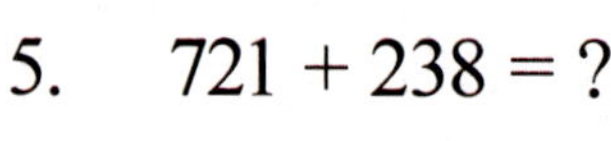

6. Count the objects in the array. Write an addition sentence to show the sum.

_____ + _____ = _____

7. I have five hundreds, four tens, and six ones. What number am I?

8. It is 3:15 now. Draw hands on the clock showing this time.

9. The following measurements were collected by a second grade classroom. Use the data to create a line plot.

Crayon Lengths

Color	Length (cm)
Sky blue	10
Orange	5
Blue-green	8
Red	7
Yellow	6
Pink	8
Purple	6
Brown	8

10. A yardstick is 36 inches long. Renee put two yardsticks end to end. How long were the two yardsticks together?

11. 33 + 19 + 11 + 21 = ?

12. What is the name of the shape?

cube   cone   cylinder

13. 35 + _____ = 80

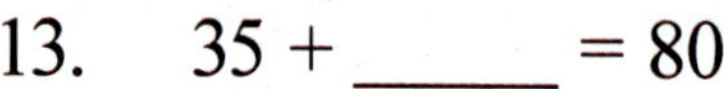

14. Todd has his morning snack at 10:00 a.m. or 10:00 p.m.?

15. How long does Arts & Crafts last?

If you went to all of the park's activities, how long would you be at the park?

Park Schedule	
Time	**Activity**
1:30 – 2:00	Story Time
2:00 – 3:30	Arts & Crafts
3:30 – 4:30	Baseball

1. 2.NBT.3	2. 2.NBT.4	3. 2.NBT.7
4. 2.OA.1	5. 2.NBT.7	6. 2.OA.4
7. 2.NBT.3	8. 2.MD.7 12 1 2 3 4 5 6 7 8 9 10 11	9. 2.MD.9 Crayon Lengths 5 6 7 8 9 10
10. 2.MD.5	11. 2.NBT.6	12. 1.G.2
13. 2.OA.1	14. 2.MD.7	15. 2.MD.10

Lesson #130

1. $64 + 29 = ?$

2. How much money is 10 quarters?

3. Write this number using base-ten numerals.
   Two hundred eight

4. Would a water bottle be 10 inches or 20 inches high?

5. Put the numbers in order from greatest to least.

   156 516 653

6. Write the name of the shape. 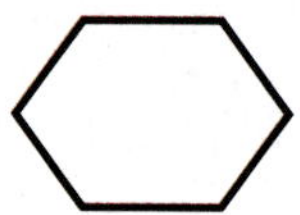

7. $635 - 324 = ?$

8. Draw a rectangle that has two equal rows and two equal columns. How many square units are in the rectangle?

9. Rocky needs two sentence strips for his project. Each strip is 7 inches long. How many inches is that all together? Write a number sentence and solve it.

10. What number comes between 257 and 430? 145 567 358

11. $425 + 361 = ?$

12. Draw 2 quadrilaterals.

13. Which shape is divided into three thirds? Draw it. 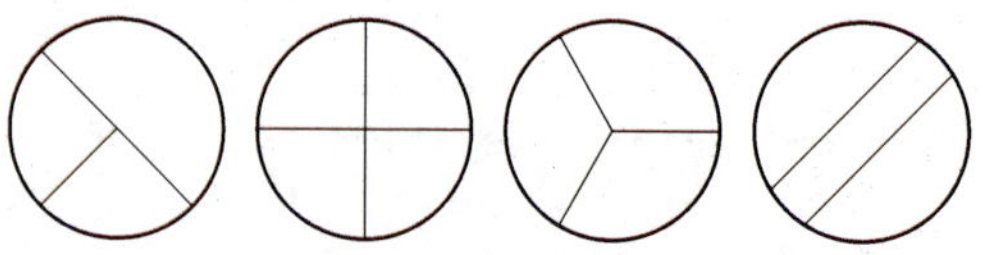

14. Turn to page 153 in your Hands On pages. Measure only the red and yellow pencils to the nearest inch. Use the data to create a line plot.

15. Kelly bought a pen for \$2.45 and a sticker book for \$1.22. How much money did she spend altogether?

1. 2.NBT.5	2. 2.MD.8	3. 2.NBT.3
4. 2.MD.3	5. 2.NBT.4	6. 2.G.1
7. 2.NBT.7	8. 2.G.2	9. 2.MD.5
10. 2.NBT.2	11. 2.NBT.7	12. 2.G.1
13. 2.G.3	14. 2.MD.3 Pencil Lengths 4 5 6 7	15. 2.MD.8

Lesson #131

1. Vince picked 17 pears on Wednesday and 25 pears on Thursday. How many more pears did Vince pick on Thursday?

2. Is 32 closer to 30 or 40?

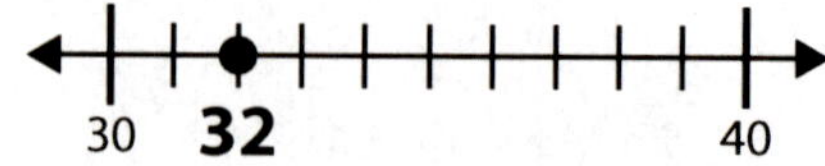

3. 466 + 421 = ?

4. Would a paperback book be closer to 7 inches or 17 inches high?

5. What base-ten number is this? 600 + 20 + 9

6. 73¢ − 25¢ = ?

7. Write the name of the figure.

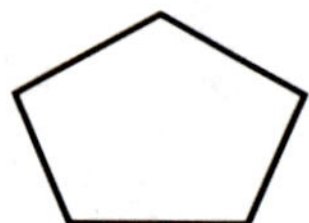

8. Fill in the sign to make this sentence true. 886 ◯ 952

9. Write your answers in centimeters.
   - How long is line M?
   - How long is line N?
   - How much longer is line M than line N?

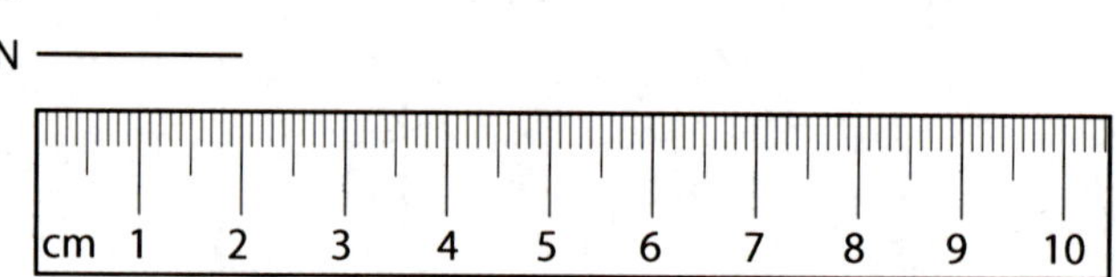

10. Which tools can you use to find out how long or wide something is? Write the words in your answer box.

    meter stick tape measure clock ruler

11. Write the base-ten number for six hundred ninety-two.

12. How much time has passed?

Start

Finish

13. 597 − 254 = ?

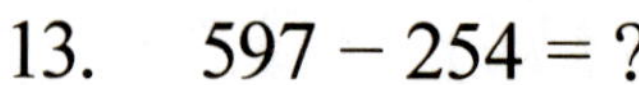

14. Draw a rectangle that has four equal rows and three equal columns. How many square units are in the rectangle?

15. Patrick spent $5.00 on popcorn. Which 2 different sizes did he buy?

A) $3.50

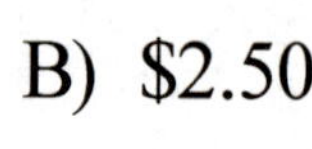
B) $2.50

C) $1.50

1. 2.OA.1	2. 3.NBT.1 (Prep)	3. 2.NBT.7
4. 2.MD.3	5. 2.NBT.3	6. 2.MD.8
7. 2.G.1	8. 2.NBT.4	9. 2.MD.4
10. 2.MD.1	11. 2.NBT.3	12. 2.MD.7
13. 2.NBT.7	14. 2.G.2	15. 2.MD.8

Lesson #132

1. Write the number using base-ten numerals. 10 + 200 + 7

2. Order these numbers from least to greatest. 865 219 713 300

3. How much money is 5 quarters?

4. \$6.55 − \$3.24 = ?

5. 257 + 641 = ?

6. Would a dollar bill be 6 inches or 16 inches long?

7. If Juan buys a pen for 90¢ and a pencil for 65¢, how much money did Juan spend altogether?

8. Draw a rectangle that has three equal rows and two equal columns. How many square units are in the rectangle?

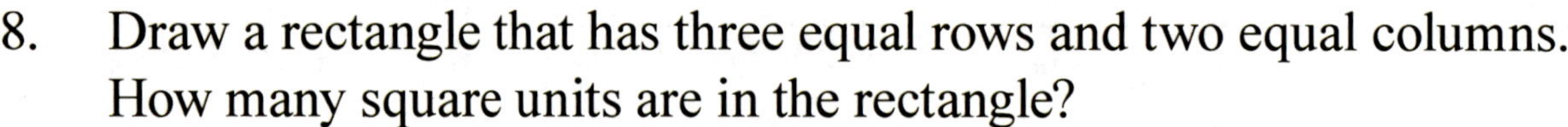

9. Write two equal addends. _____ + _____ = 16

10. Nicki's number is nine less than 29. What is Nicki's number?

11. **This shape is a *rectangular prism*. It looks like a brick.** Write rectangular prism in the box.

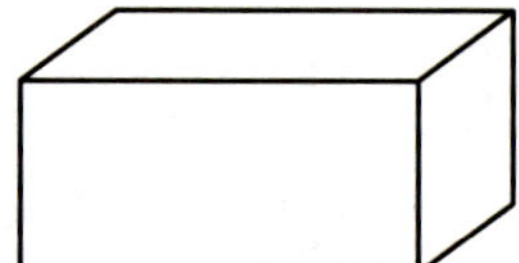

12 – 15. Daphne asked her friends about their favorite hotdog toppings. Use the information in Daphne's data chart to make a bar graph. (See the *Help Pages*.)

- Give the graph a title.
- Fill in the numbers for the left side of the graph. Zero is given. Go up by 1s.
- Write labels on the left side and bottom of the graph.
- Draw the bars to the correct height. Label each bar.

Type of Topping	# of Votes
Ketchup	4
Mustard	6
Relish	2

1. 2.NBT.3

2. 2.NBT.4

3. 2.MD.8

4. 2.MD.8

5. 2.NBT.7

6. 2.MD.3

7. 2.MD.8

8. 2.G.2

9. 2.OA.3

10. 2.OA.1

11. 1.G.2

12 – 15. 2.MD.10

0

Lesson #133

1. What number is 100 less than 762?

2. Is the number of suns even or odd? Count by 2s.

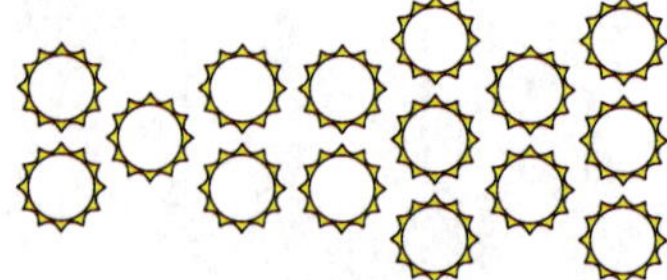

3. Write this as a base-ten numeral. 5 ones, 8 tens, and 1 hundred

4. If you have a quarter, a nickel, and twelve pennies, how many cents do you have?

5. What is the name of this shape?

   cube   rectangular prism   cone

6. I have 6 hundreds, 9 tens and 3 ones. What number am I?

7. Fill in the sign to make this sentence true. 352 ◯ 624

8. Draw a rectangle that has four equal rows and four equal columns. How many square units are in the rectangle?

9. Count the objects in the array. Write an addition sentence to show the sum.

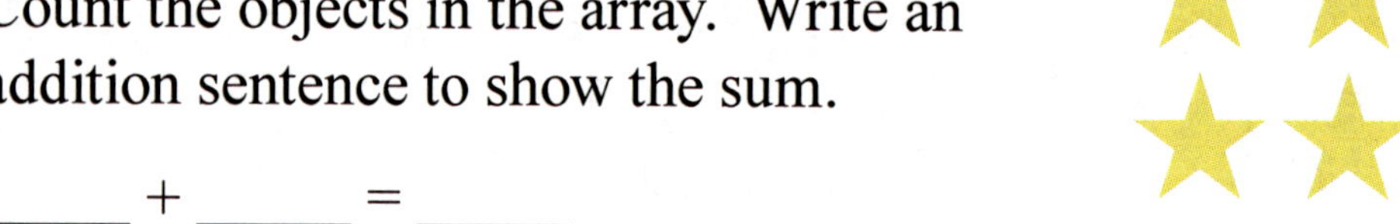

   _____ + _____ = _____

10. Write your answers in centimeters.
    - How long is line X?
    - How long is line Y?
    - How much shorter is line Y than line X?

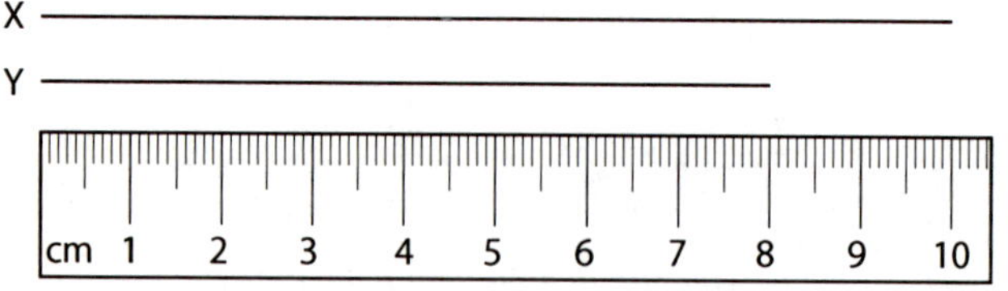

11. There are two bicycles in Mr. Hanson's garage. One bike is 24 inches wide. The other bicycle is 30 inches wide. Will the bicycles fit end to end in a space that is 50 inches wide?

12. 446 + 353 = ?

13. 835 − 313 = ?

14. 18 + 36 + 14 = ?

15. 5 + 8 = ?

1. 2.NBT.8	2. 2.OA.3	3. 2.NBT.3
4. 2.MD.8	5. 1.G.2	6. 2.NBT.3
7. 2.NBT.4	8. 2.G.2	9. 2.OA.4
10. 2.MD.4	11. 2.MD.5	12. 2.NBT.7
13. 2.NBT.7	14. 2.NBT.6	15. 2.OA.2

Lesson #134

1. If you have twenty-one nickels,
do you have more or less than one dollar?

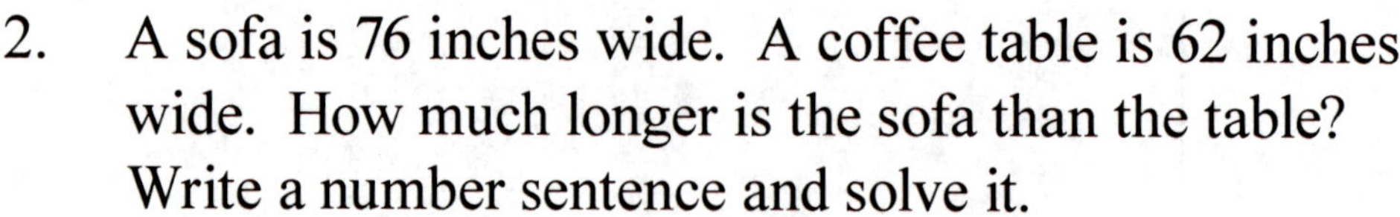

2. A sofa is 76 inches wide. A coffee table is 62 inches wide. How much longer is the sofa than the table? Write a number sentence and solve it.

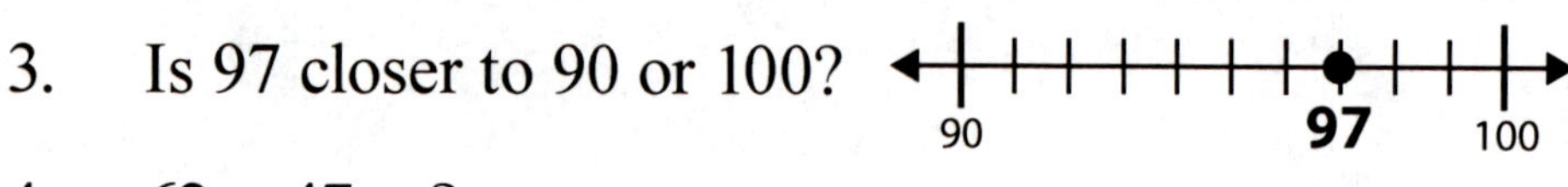

3. Is 97 closer to 90 or 100?

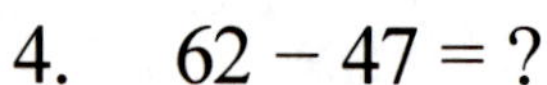

4. 62 − 47 = ?

5. 366 + 431= ?

6. There were 37 birds in a tree. As a cat walked toward the tree, 18 of the birds flew away. How many birds are still in the tree?

7. Write two equal addends. _____ + _____ = 18

8. Fill in the sign to make this sentence true. 478 ◯ 465

9. Draw a rectangle that has two equal rows and three equal columns. How many square units are in the rectangle?

10. Write the number using base-ten numerals. 45 tens

11. Count by fives. 85, ____, ____, 100, ____

12. Shane's number is 40 less than 90.
What is Shane's number?

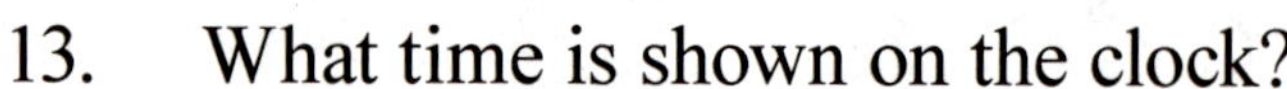

13. What time is shown on the clock?

14. Which is greater, 7 dimes or $1.00?

15. Mason set up a lemonade stand. He sold 20 glasses of lemonade in the morning, 25 glasses of lemonade at lunchtime, and 30 glasses of lemonade at dinnertime. How many glasses of lemonade did Mason sell all together? Write a number sentence and solve it.

1. 2.MD.8	2. 2.MD.5	3. 3.NBT.1 (Prep)
4. 2.NBT.5	5. 2.NBT.7	6. 2.OA.1
7. 2.OA.3	8. 2.NBT.4	9. 2.G.2
10. 2.NBT.3	11. 2.NBT.2	12. 2.OA.1
13. 2.MD.7	14. 2.MD.8	15. 2.OA.1

Lesson #135

1. Count the objects in the array. Write an addition sentence to show the sum.

   _____ + _____ + _____ + _____ + _____ = _____

2. Peggy has three quarters and two nickels. Nicki has a dollar bill. Who has more money, Peggy or Nicki?

3. Turn to page 153 in your Hands On pages. Measure all the pencils except the yellow pencils to the nearest inch. Use the data to create a line plot.

4. Dana and Leo joined a book club. Dana read 22 pages yesterday and 11 pages today. Leo read 14 pages yesterday and 16 pages today. Who read more pages, Dana or Leo?

5. 6 + 9 = ?

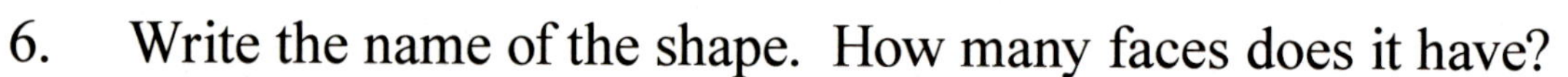

6. Write the name of the shape. How many faces does it have?

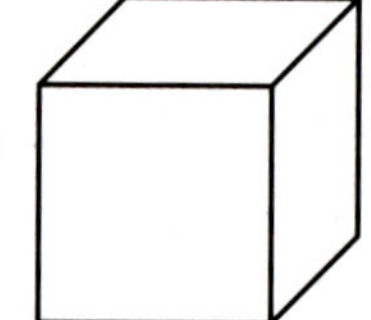

7. Fill in the sign to make this sentence true. 342 ◯ 856

8. The difference is the answer to a(n) ________ problem.

9. How much time has passed?

10. 706 − 405 = ?

11. Write this as a base-ten numeral. 7 hundreds, 6 ones, and 1 ten

12. Mentally add 100. 146, 246, _____, _____, _____, 646

13. Write your answers in centimeters.
    - How long is line Y? Y ———————
    - How long is line Z? Z ——————————————————
    - How much shorter is line Y than line Z?

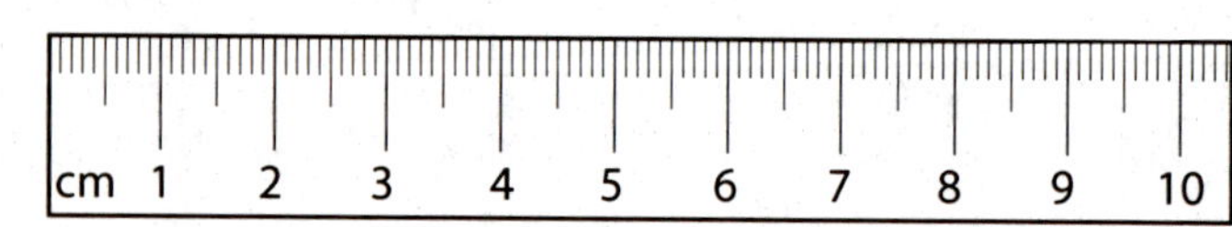

14. What number is 100 more than 125?

15. Which shape is divided into three thirds? Draw it.

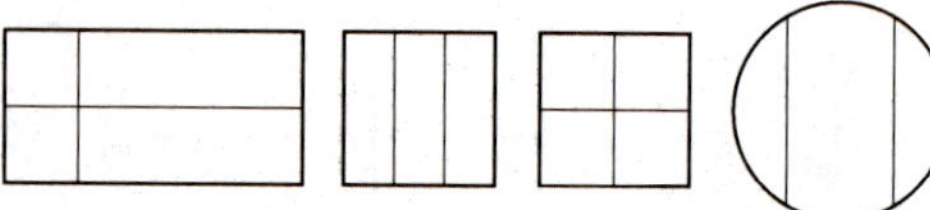

1. 2.OA.4	2. 2.MD.8	3. 2.MD.3 Pencil Lengths 4 5 6 7
4. 2.OA.1	5. 2.OA.2	6. 2.G.1
7. 2.NBT.4	8. 1.OA.7	9. 2.MD.7
10. 2.NBT.7	11. 2.NBT.3	12. 2.NBT.8
13. 2.MD.4	14. 2.NBT.8	15. 2.G.3

Lesson #136

1. Write 653 using words.

2. What is the name of this shape?

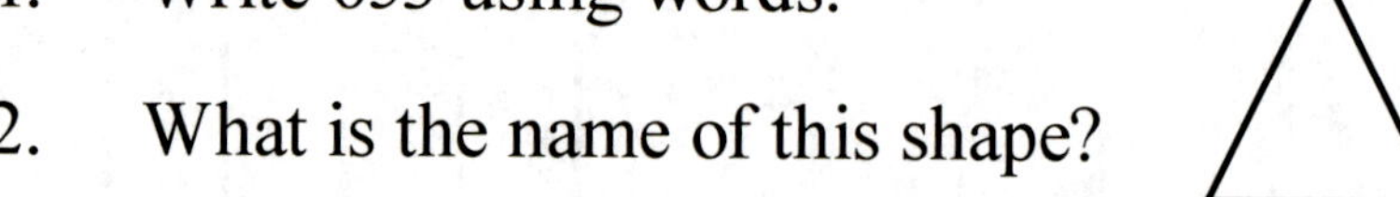

3. Write the number using base-ten numerals.　67 tens

4. Rainey, Frank, and Jana each have a desk that is 24 inches wide. If the three students put their desks side by side, how many inches long would the line of desks be? Write a number sentence.

5. If you have four dollar bills, four quarters, and ten pennies, do you have more or less than five dollars?

6. Draw a rectangle that has five equal rows and five equal columns. How many square units are in the rectangle?

7. Count the objects in the array. Write an addition sentence to show the sum.

_____ + _____ = _____

8. Write two equal addends. _____ + _____ = 6

9. Fill in the sign to make this sentence true.　862 ○ 799

10. 935 – 623 = ?

11. What time is shown on the clock?

12. 518 + 271 = ?

13. The number 600 has _____ hundreds, _____ tens, and _____ ones.

14. There were 48 worms in Jason's worm farm. He sold 12 worms to Jerry. How many worms did Jason have left?

15. How many total insects were in the yard?

How many more ants than grasshoppers were there?

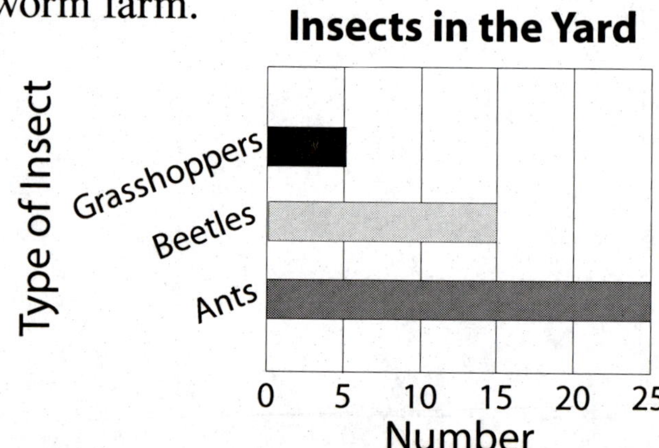

1. 2.NBT.3	2. 2.G.1	3. 2.NBT.3
4. 2.MD.5	5. 2.MD.8	6. 2.G.2
7. 2.OA.4	8. 2.OA.3	9. 2.NBT.4
10. 2.NBT.7	11. 2.MD.7	12. 2.NBT.7
13. 2.NBT.1	14. 2.OA.1	15. 2.MD.10

Lesson #137

1. I have three hundreds, two tens, and five ones. What number am I?

2. Draw a rectangle that has two equal rows and four equal columns. How many square units are in the rectangle?

3. Count the objects in the array. Write an addition sentence to show the sum.

   _____ + _____ + _____ + _____ = _____

4. 637 − 426 = ?

5. 35 + 21 + 13 = ?

6. How much time has passed?

Start

Finish

7. Write 734 using words.

8. The answer to a subtraction problem is the ________.

9. Eight quarters are the same amount of money as two ________.

10. How many sides and angles does a hexagon have?

11. Order these numbers from greatest to least.

    455   231   786   239

12 – 15. Marty spent a week counting the birds he saw most often. Use the information in Marty's data chart to make a bar graph. (See the *Help Pages*.)

- Give the graph a title.
- Fill in the numbers for the left side of the graph. Zero is given. Go up by 1s.
- Write labels on the left side and bottom of the graph.
- Draw the bars to the correct height. Label each bar.

Type of Bird	# of Views
Blue Jay	2
Sparrow	1
Robin	6

1. 2.NBT.3	2. 2.G.2	3. 2.OA.4
4. 2.NBT.7	5. 2.NBT.6	6. 2.MD.7
7. 2.NBT.3	8. 1.OA.7	9. 2.MD.8
10. 2.G.1	12 – 15. 2.MD.10	
11. 2.NBT.4		

0

Lesson #138

1. A hiking trail is 56 miles long. The scouts hiked 21 miles the first day and 23 miles the second day. How many more miles until the scouts reach the end of the trail?

2. 834 + 44 = ?

3. What number comes just before 1,000?

4. What base-ten number is this? 700 + 30 + 8

5. Order the numbers from least to greatest.

   475 199 156 516

6. Turn to page 153 in your Hands On pages. Measure pencils C–M to the nearest inch. Use the data to create a line plot.

7. Write the time shown on the clock.

8. 724 − 513 = ?

9. A shape that has four sides and four angles is called a ________.

   quadrilateral pentagon triangle

10. Nolan has a dollar and 68¢. Lance has five quarters and two dimes. Who has more money, Nolan or Lance?

11. The merry-go-round can hold 36 people. When the ride started, 34 people got on. At the first stop, 14 got off and 13 people got on. How many were on the merry-go-round then?

12. Write your answers in centimeters.
    - How long is line A?
    - How long is line B?
    - How much longer is line B than line A?

A
B

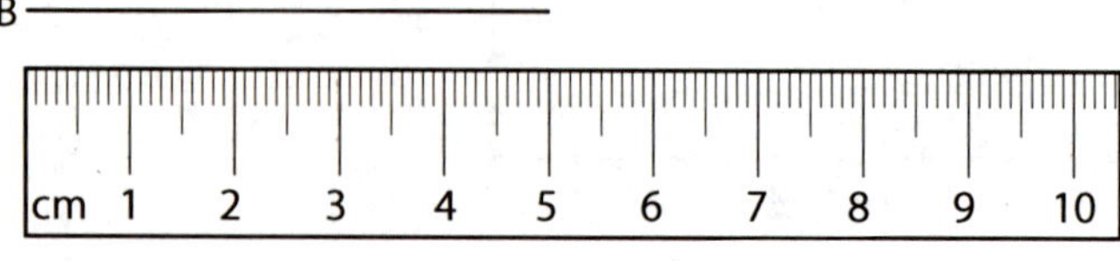

13. Fill in the sign to make this sentence true. 268 ○ 199

14. How much of the circle is shaded?

    half a third a fourth all

15. Write 985 using words.

1. 2.MD.5	2. 2.NBT.7	3. 2.NBT.2
4. 2.NBT.3	5. 2.NBT.4	6. 2.MD.3 Pencil Lengths (inches) 4 5 6 7
7. 2.MD.7	8. 2.NBT.7	9. 2.G.1
10. 2.MD.8	11. 2.OA.1	12. 2.MD.4
13. 2.NBT.4	14. 2.G.3	15. 2.NBT.3

Lesson #139

1. Is 28 closer to 20 or 30?

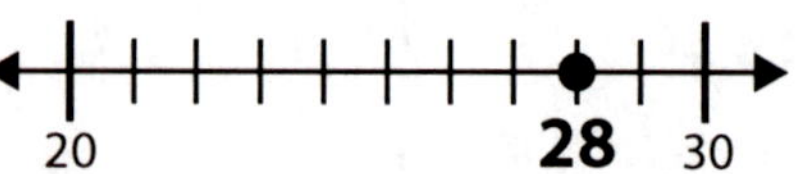

2. 843 − 332 = ?

3. In the answer box, circle the grid that has 20 square units.

4. A number has 6 hundreds, 5 tens and 4 ones. What is the number?

5. Turn to page 153 in your Hands On pages. Measure pencils A–H to the nearest inch. Use the data to create a line plot.

6. Fill in the sign to make this sentence true. 416 ◯ 146

7. Mentally add 100. 312, 412, _____, _____, 712, _____, 912

8. The second grade classes are collecting aluminum cans for recycling. Ms. Rita's class collected 25 cans, Mr. Walker's class collected 39 cans, and Ms. Stewart's class collected 35 cans. How many cans were collected?

9. If you have seven nickels, three dimes, and four pennies do you have more or less than one dollar?

10. 538 + 261 = ?

11. Count the objects in the array. Write an addition sentence to show the sum.

12. 16 + 15 + 14 + 13 = ?

13. The cherry tree grew 16 centimeters one year and 11 centimeters the next year. How many centimeters did the cherry tree grow in two years? Write a number sentence to find the answer.

14. Was Ginny's birthday cake almost 15 centimeters or 40 centimeters tall?

15. What number does the symbol stand for? 10 + ◆ = 35

1. 3.NBT.1 (Prep)	2. 2.NBT.7	3. 2.G.2
4. 2.NBT.3	5. 2.MD.3 Pencil Lengths (inches) 4 5 6 7	6. 2.NBT.4
7. 2.NBT.8	8. 2.OA.1	9. 2.MD.8
10. 2.NBT.7	11. 2.OA.4	12. 2.NBT.6
13. 2.MD.5	14. 2.MD.3	15. 2.OA.1

Lesson #140

1. Write your answers in centimeters.
   - How long is A?
   - How long is B?
   - How much shorter is A than B?

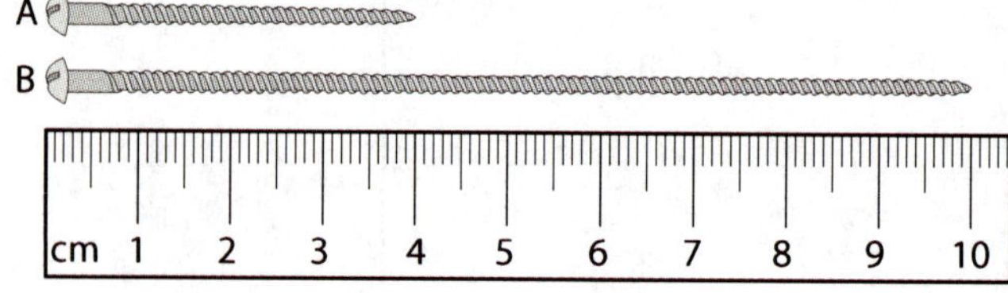

2. 585 + 304 = ?
3. Is this figure a cone?
4. Count by tens. 340, 350, ____, ____, ____
5. Mrs. Sharp has 48 pencils. There are 32 students in the class. If every student gets a pencil, how many pencils will be left over?

6. What time is it?
7. \$2.85 – \$1.35 = ?
8. Fill in the sign to make this sentence true. 314 ◯ 143
9. Write this as a base-ten numeral. One hundred thirty-seven
10. In the answer box, circle the grid that has 16 square units.
11. What number is 100 less than 347?
12. Count the objects in the array. Write an addition statement to show the sum.

13. Twenty nickels are the same amount of money as one __________.
14. Which tools can you use to find out how long or wide something is? Write the words in your answer box.

    yardstick　　scale　　ruler　　air pump

15. There are 47 students in the school band. Twenty-three students play a wind instrument. How many students do <u>not</u> play a wind instrument?

1. 2.MD.4	2. 2.NBT.7	3. 2.G.1
4. 2.NBT.2	5. 2.OA.1	6. 2.MD.7
7. 2.MD.8	8. 2.NBT.4	9. 2.NBT.3
10. 2.G.2	11. 2.NBT.8	12. 2.OA.4
13. 2.MD.8	14. 2.MD.1	15. 2.OA.1

Common Core Mathematics 2

Help Pages

Help Pages

Vocabulary

Arithmetic Operations

Addition → When you combine numbers, you add. The sign "+" means add. The answer to an addition problem is called the *sum*.
Example: When you combine 5 and 2, the sum is 7; 5 + 2 = 7.

Subtraction → When you take one number away from another, you subtract. The sign "–" means subtract. The answer to a subtraction problem is called the *difference*. **Example**: When you take 1 away from 5, the difference is 4; 5 – 1 = 4.

Geometry - Shapes (Two-dimensional)

Number of Sides	Name	Number of Sides	Name
3 △	Triangle	4 ▭	Quadrilateral
5 ⬠	Pentagon	6 ⬡	Hexagon

Geometry - Solids (Three-dimensional)

Cone —	Rectangular Prism —
Cube —	Sphere —
Cylinder —	

Help Pages

Geometry - Shapes and their Attributes

Cube faces

Any side of a three-dimensional shape is called a face. A cube has six faces: top, bottom, front, back, left side, and right side. Each face of a cube looks like a square.

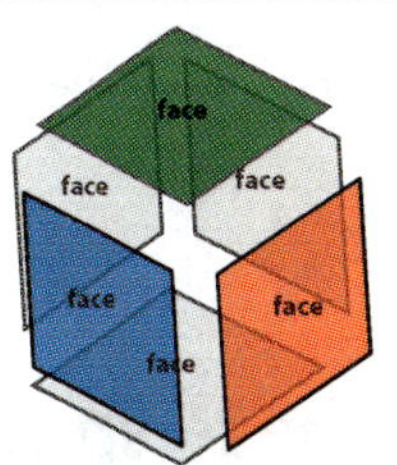

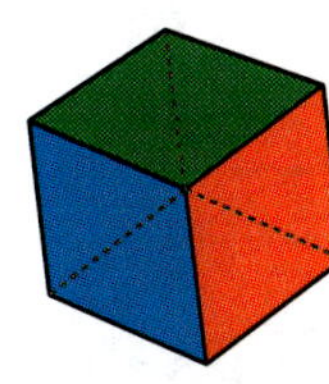

Grid paper

In this book, grids are included in the answer boxes to help you draw a rectangle. Use the grid paper to help you show equal rows and equal columns inside the rectangle.

Example: Draw a rectangle having three equal rows and two equal columns. Find the total number of square units.

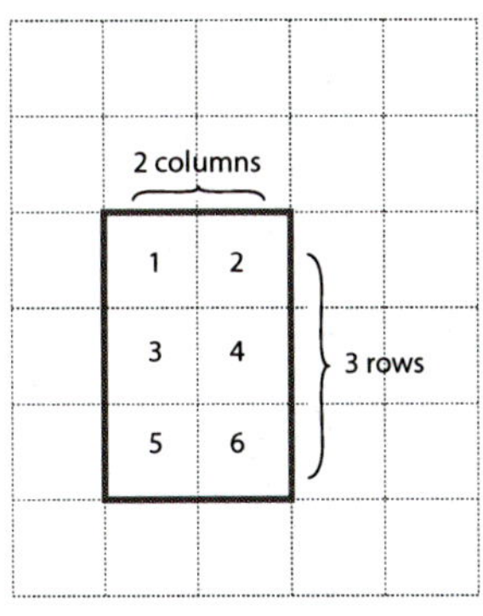

This rectangle has a total of 6 square units.

Arrays

An **array** shows objects in equal rows and equal columns.

This array has four rows of three caterpillars.
Four groups of three are equal to twelve.
3 + 3 + 3 + 3 = 12

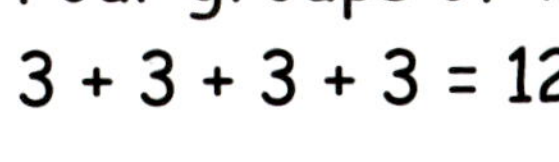

This array has three rows of four ladybugs.
Three groups of four are equal to twelve.
4 + 4 + 4 = 12

Help Pages

Solved Examples

Equal Shares

This box has 4 equal shares or parts.
One fourth is shaded.

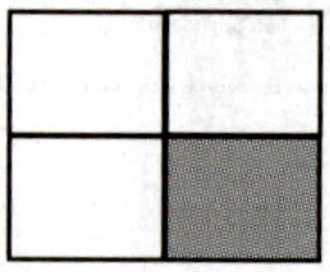

Each of these shapes shows two halves.

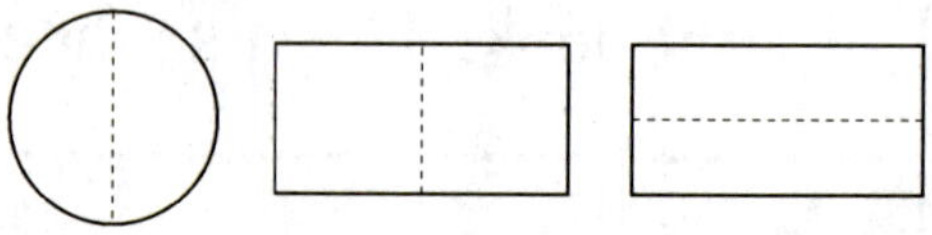

Each of these shapes shows three thirds.

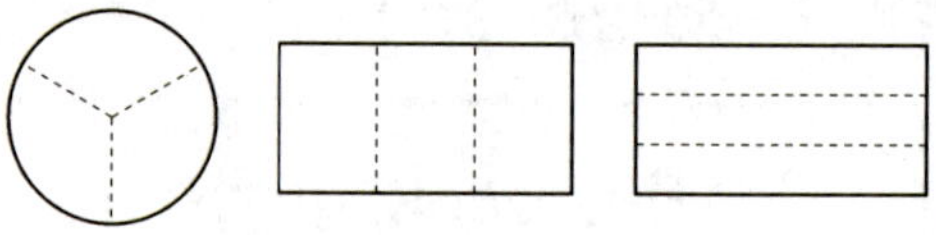

Each of these shapes shows four fourths.

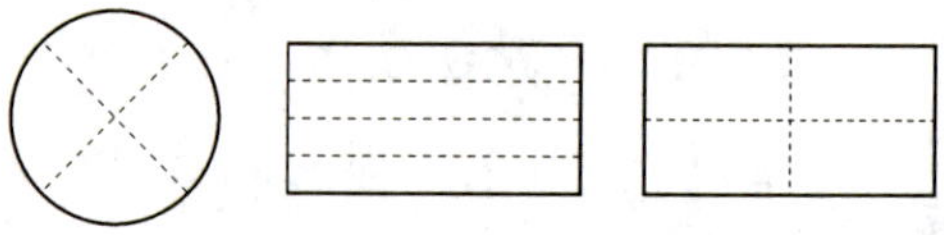

Greater Than and Less Than

Numbers can be compared by saying one is **greater than** another or one is **less than** another.

The symbol "**>**" means *greater than.* The symbol "**<**" means *less than.* Think of the wide part of the sign as an alligator's mouth eating the bigger number. (Hint: The open part of the sign is near the bigger number.)

Examples:

12 is less than 25 — 12 25 — 12 < 25

31 is greater than 16 — 31 16 — 31 > 16

Help Pages

Solved Examples

Place Value

1,	0	0	0
Thousands	Hundreds	Tens	Ones

The number above is read:
one thousand

4	0	5
Hundreds	Tens	Ones

The number above is read:
four hundred five.

Fact Family

A **fact family** is a set of related facts using addition, subtraction, and the same three numbers.

Example: Write a fact family using 3, 4, and 7.

3 + 4 = 7　　7 − 3 = 4
4 + 3 = 7　　7 − 4 = 3

Base-Ten Numbers

Base-ten numbers can be named in many ways.

Example: These expanded forms all name 234.

two hundred thirty-four

2 hundreds, 3 tens, 4 ones

3 tens, 4 ones, 2 hundreds

234 ones

2 hundreds, 34 ones

23 tens, 4 ones

200 + 30 + 4

Help Pages

Solved Examples

Whole Numbers

When adding or subtracting whole numbers, first the numbers must be lined-up from the right. Starting with the ones place, add (or subtract) the numbers. When adding, if the answer has 2 digits, write the ones digit and regroup the tens digit. For subtraction, it may also be necessary to regroup first. Then, add (or subtract) the numbers in the tens place. Continue with the hundreds, etc.

Look at these examples of **addition**.

Examples: Find the sum of 314 and 12. Add 648 and 236.

$$\begin{array}{r} 314 \\ +\ 12 \\ \hline 326 \end{array}$$

1. Line up the numbers on the right.
2. Beginning with the ones place, add. Regroup if necessary.
3. Repeat with the tens place.
4. Continue this process with the hundreds place, etc.

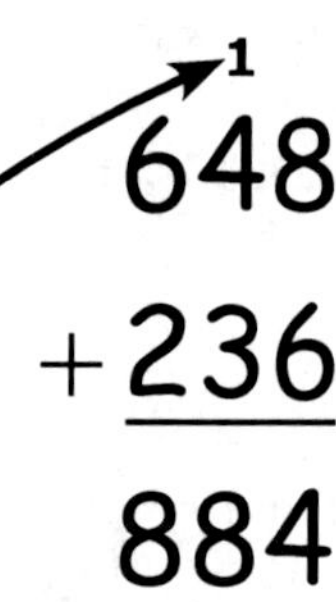

Use the following examples of **subtraction** to help you.

Example: Subtract 37 from 93.

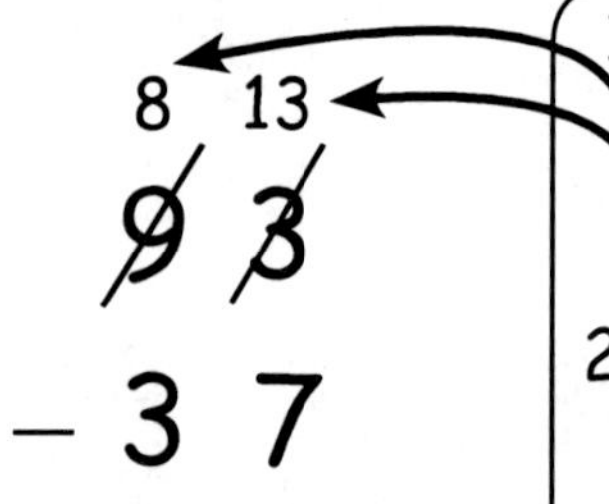

1. Begin with the ones place. Check to see if you need to regroup. Since 7 is larger than 3, you must regroup to 8 tens and 13 ones.
2. Now look at the tens place. Check to see if you need to regroup. Since 3 is less than 8, you do not need to regroup.
3. Subtract each place value beginning with the ones.

Help Pages

Solved Examples

Whole Numbers (continued)

Example: Find the difference of 425 and 233.

```
  3 12
  4̸ 2̸ 5
– 2 3 3
-------
  1 9 2
```

1. Begin with the ones place. Check to see if you need to regroup. Since 3 is less than 5, you do not need to regroup.
2. Now look at the tens place. Check to see if you need to regroup. Since 3 is larger than 2, you must regroup to 3 hundreds and 12 tens.
3. Now look at the hundreds place. Check to see if you need to regroup. Since 2 is less than 3, you are ready to subtract.
4. Subtract each place value beginning with the ones.

Sometimes when doing subtraction, you must **subtract from zero**. You will always need to regroup. Use the examples below to help you.

Example: Subtract 38 from 60.

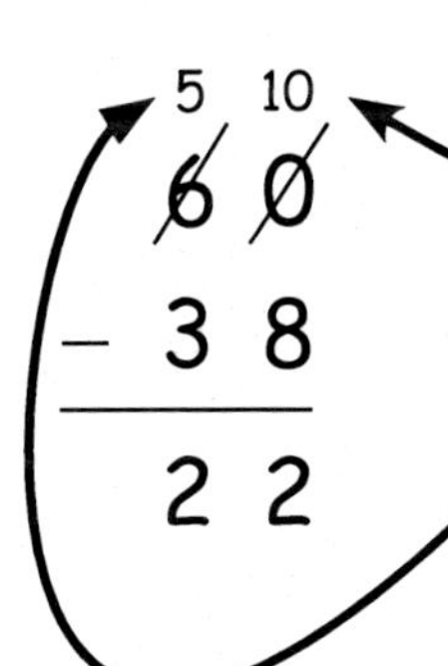

1. Begin with the ones place. Since 8 is more than 0, you must regroup.
2. Regroup to 5 tens and 10 ones.
3. Then, subtract each place value beginning with the ones.

Example: Find the difference between 500 and 261.

```
      9
  4  1̸0̸ 10
  5̸  0̸  0̸
– 2  6  1
---------
  2  3  9
```

Help Pages

Solved Examples

Number Lines

Number lines can help us find sums and differences.

Example: Use the number line to show the sum of 9 + 9.

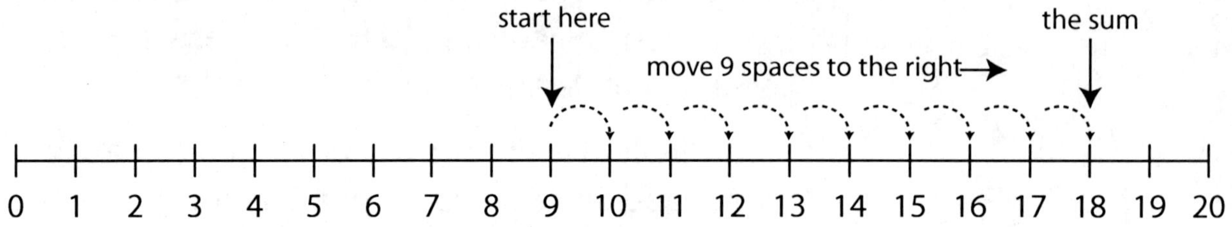

Start at the first number (9), then **add 9** (go to the right 9 spaces). You end up at 18 (the sum).

Example: Use the number line to show the difference of 36 – 7.

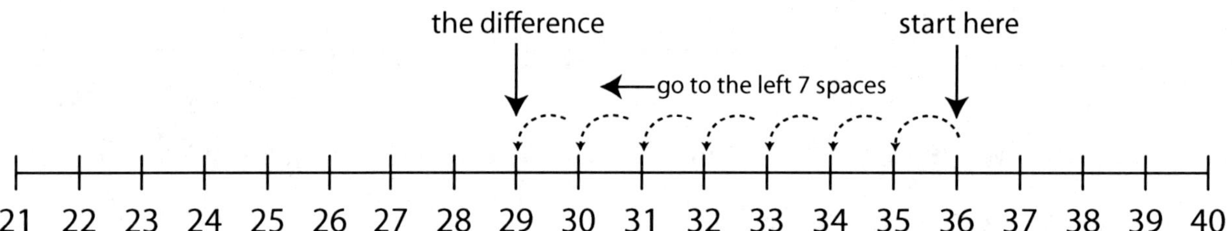

Start at the first number (36), then **subtract 7** (go to the left 7 spaces). You end up at 29 (the difference).

Help Pages

Solved Examples

Graphs

On a **line plot** you can quickly see data. It may be spread out or close together.

To make a line plot,

- Give the line plot a title.
- Find the greatest value and the lowest value in the set of data.
- Draw a number line on the grid paper near the bottom. The number line should begin with the lowest value you found.
- The length of your line should include space to mark from your lowest to your greatest value.
- For each piece of data, draw an "x" above the matching value. An "x" on the line plot will take the place of each number from the data chart. No student names are needed.

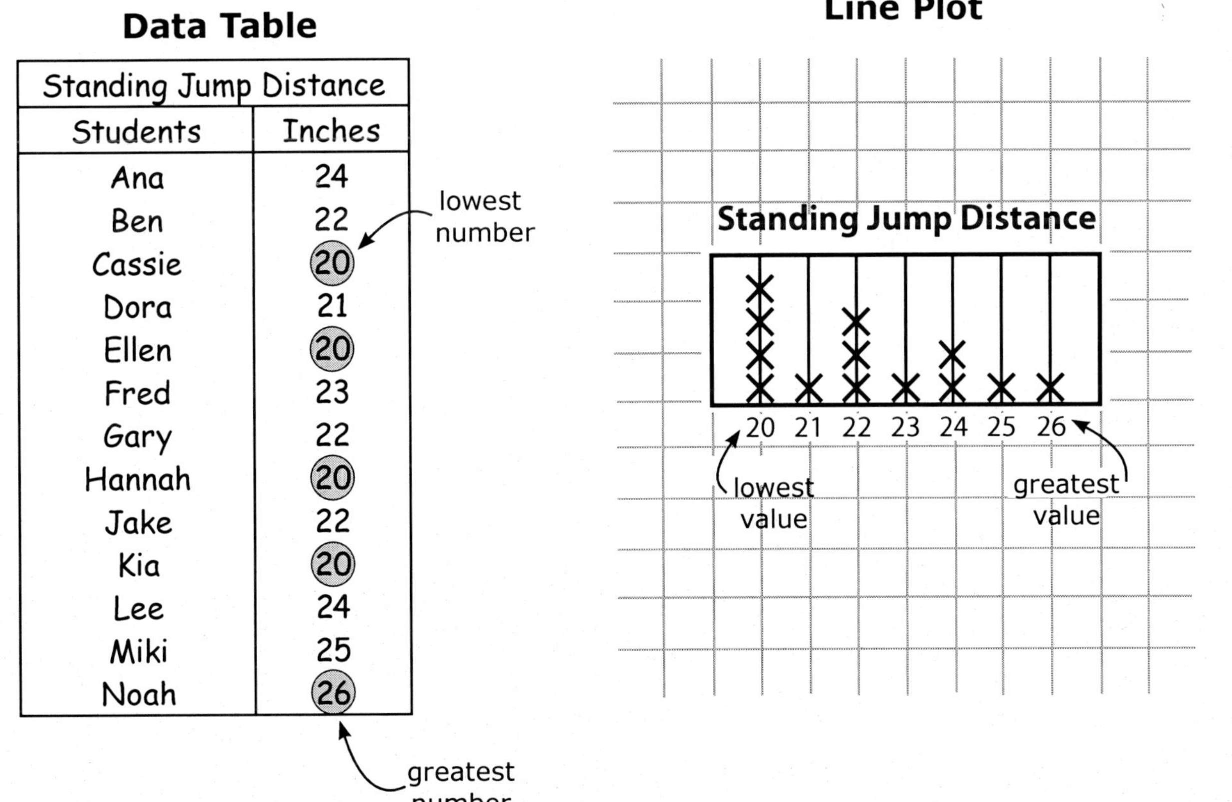

Help Pages

Solved Examples

Graphs (continued)

Picture graphs use pictures or symbols to show and compare data. The survey results in the chart below can be shown on a picture graph.

Terri asked 45 people to vote for a favorite kind of music. First, she made a survey chart to show how people voted. Then, Terri made a picture graph to show how people voted.

Here is how to make a picture graph:

- Give labels to the two sides of the graph. The labels on Terri's graph are Kinds of Music and Number of Votes.
- Choose a symbol for your data and draw it in a key. This graph shows that one smiley face stands for 1 vote .
- Draw the correct number of symbols next to each item.
- Give the graph a title.

Survey Chart

Favorite Music	
Kind of Music	Number of Votes
Country	6
Hip Hop	10
Latin	8
Pop	12
R & B	9

Picture Graph

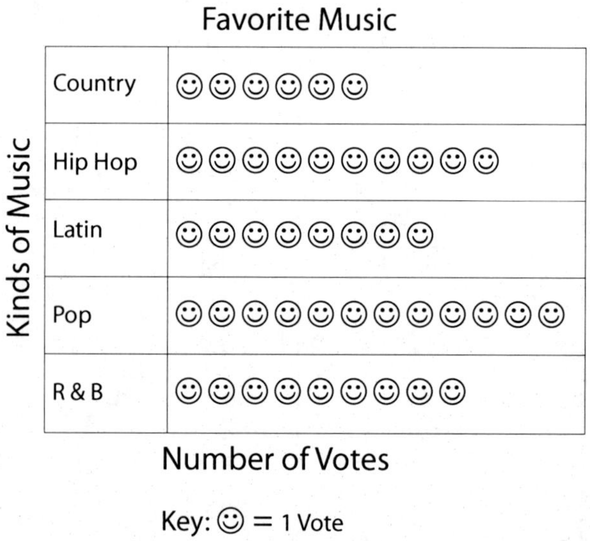

Favorite Music

Kinds of Music	Number of Votes
Country	☺☺☺☺☺☺
Hip Hop	☺☺☺☺☺☺☺☺☺☺
Latin	☺☺☺☺☺☺☺☺
Pop	☺☺☺☺☺☺☺☺☺☺☺☺
R & B	☺☺☺☺☺☺☺☺☺

Key: ☺ = 1 Vote

Help Pages

Solved Examples

Graphs (continued)

A **bar graph** is another way to show and compare data.

Terri can show her data on a bar graph.

Here is how to make one:

- Give labels to the two sides of the graph (called a horizontal axis and a vertical axis).
- Choose a simple scale for the vertical axis. Start at 0 and go up by 1 or another easy number. This graph goes up by 2.
- Write the kinds of music on the horizontal axis.
- Draw and color in each bar to a height on the graph that matches the number in the survey chart.

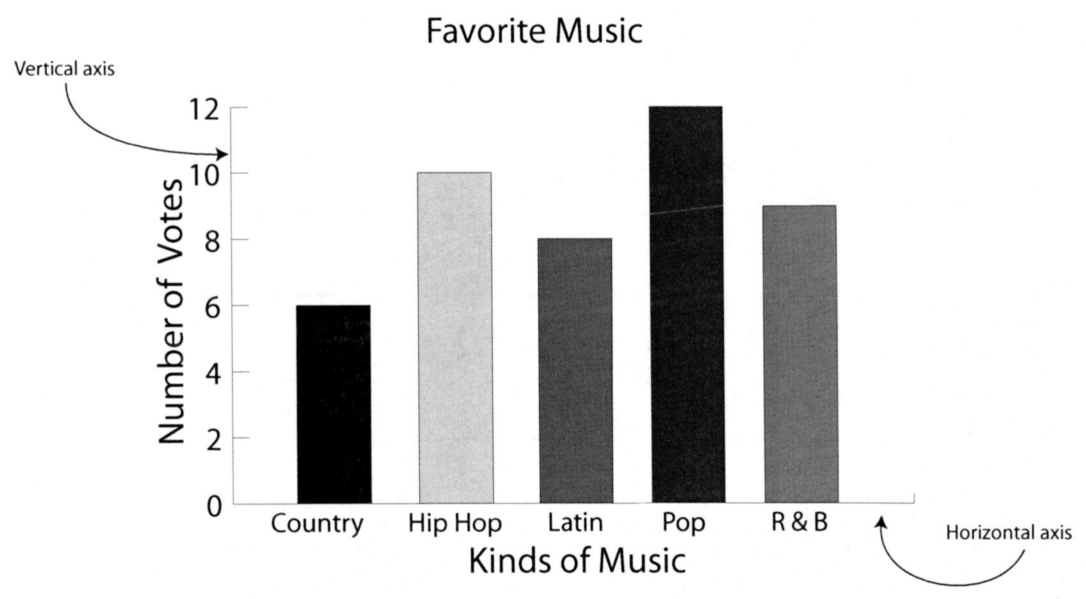

Help Pages

Solved Examples

Coins

The two sides of 4 coins are shown here.

A **penny** is worth 1¢.  

  A **nickel** is worth 5¢.

A **dime** is worth 10¢.  

  A **quarter** is worth 25¢.

Measurement – Relationships

Time	Distance
30 minutes = 1 half-hour	12 inches = 1 foot
60 minutes = 1 hour	100 centimeters = 1 meter

Help Pages

Solved Examples

Time

The measure of how long something takes to happen is called **elapsed time**.

Example:

The movie began at 7:00 and ended at 9:00.

How long did the movie last? (How much time passed between 7:00 and 9:00?) There are **2 hours** between 7:00 and 9:00.

Example:

How many hours pass from the beginning of Spelling class until the end of Math class?

Class Schedule

8:30 – 9:00	Spelling
9:00 – 10:00	Reading
10:00 – 11:30	Math
11:30 – 12:00	English

Spelling starts at 8:30. Math ends at 11:30. (How much time passes between 8:30 and 11:30?)

There are **3 hours** between 8:30 and 11:30.

Hands-On Pages

Hands-On Pages

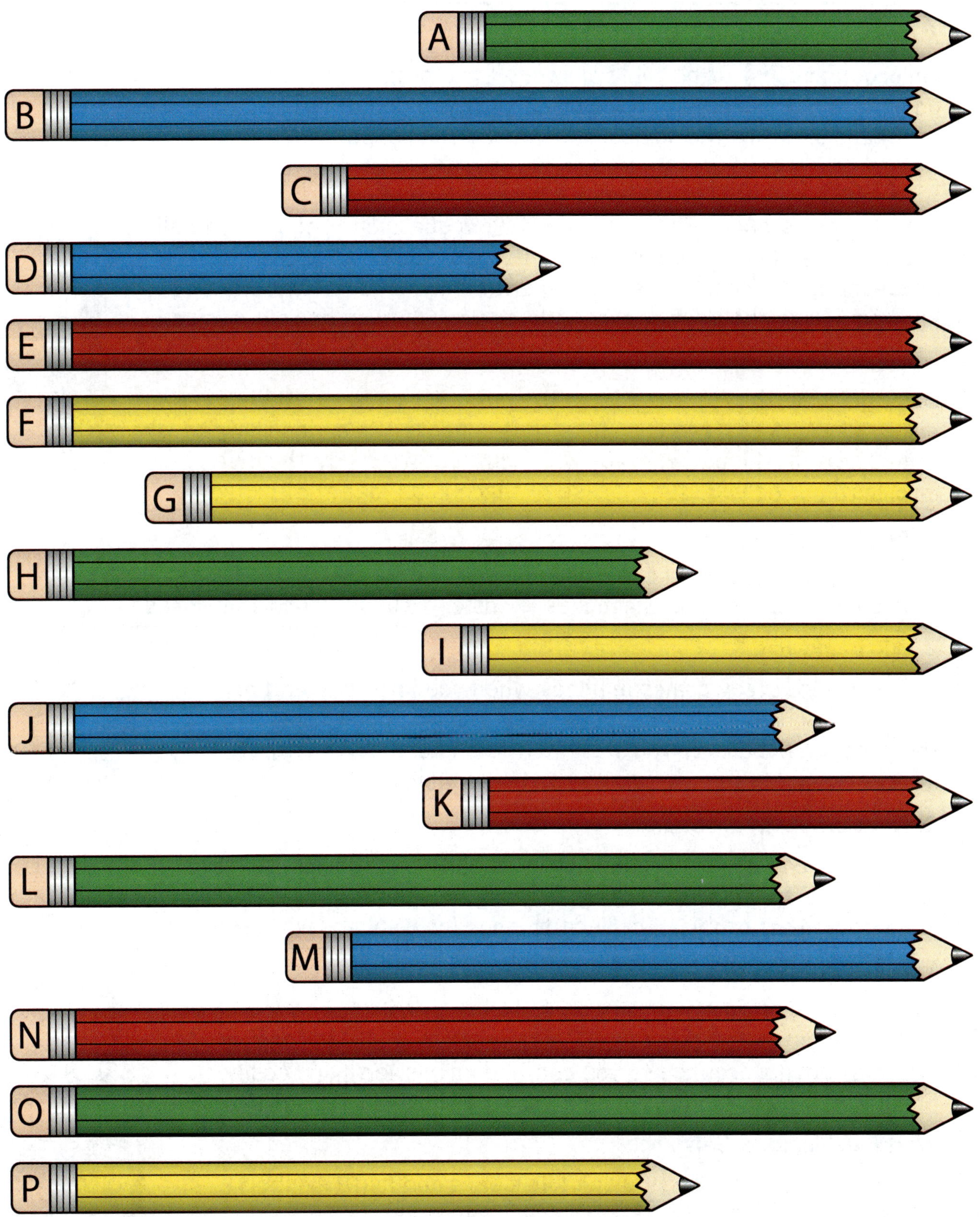

Problem Solving Strategies

Make an Organized List

An **organized list** of possible answers for a problem uses an order that makes sense to you so that you do not miss any ideas or write the same answer more than once.

Guess and Check

For the **guess and check** strategy, take a guess and see if it fits all the clues by checking each one. If it does, you have solved the problem. If it doesn't, keep trying until it works out. One way to know you have the best answer is when your answer fits every clue.

Look for a Pattern

Sometimes math problems ask us to *continue a pattern by writing what comes next*. A **pattern** is an idea that repeats. In order to write what comes next in the pattern, you will first need to study the given information. As you study it, see if there is an idea that repeats.

Draw a Picture

When you **draw a picture** it helps you see the ideas you are trying to understand. The picture makes it easier to understand the words.

Work Backward

Using this strategy comes in handy when you know the end of a problem and the steps along the way, but you don't know how the problem began. If you start at the end and do the steps in reverse order you will end up at the beginning.

Solve a Simpler Problem

When you read a math problem with ideas that seem too big to understand, try to **solve a simpler problem**. Instead of giving up or skipping that problem, replace the harder numbers with easier ones.

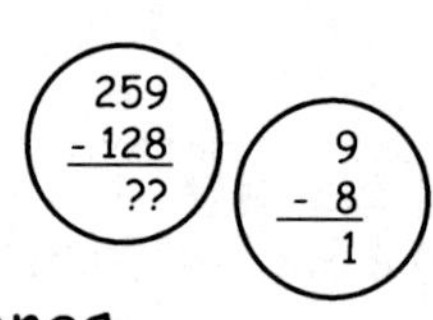

Make a Table

Tables have columns and rows. Labels are helpful too. Writing your ideas in this type of table (or chart) can help you organize the information in a problem so you can find an answer more easily. Sometimes it will make a pattern show up that you did not see before.

Write a Number Sentence

A **number sentence** is made up of numbers and math symbols (+ − × ÷ > < =). To use this strategy you will turn the words of a problem into numbers and symbols.

Problem Solving Strategies (continued)

Use Logical Reasoning

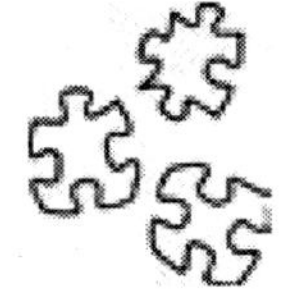

Logical reasoning is basically common sense. **Logical** means "sensible." **Reasoning** is "a way of thinking." **Logical reasoning** is done one step at a time until you see the whole answer.

Make a Model

A **model** can be a picture you draw, or an object you make or find to **help you understand the words** of a problem. These objects can be coins, paper clips, paper for folding, or cubes.